origami transport

35 origami cars, trains, boats, planes, and more

mari ono

CICO BOOKS

This edition published in 2025 by CICO Books
An imprint of Ryland Peters & Small Ltd
20–21 Jockey's Fields   1452 Davis Bugg Road
London WC1R 4BW   Warrenton, NC 27589

www.rylandpeters.com
Email: euregulations@rylandpeters.com

10 9 8 7 6 5 4 3 2 1

First published in 2014 as *Origami Cars, Boats, Trains, and More*

Text © Mari Ono 2014, 2025
Design and photography © CICO Books 2014, 2025

The designs in this book are copyright and must not be made for sale.

The author's moral rights have been asserted. All rights reserved. No part of this publication may be reproduced, stored in a retrieval system, or transmitted in any form or by any means, electronic, mechanical, photocopying, or otherwise, without the prior permission of the publisher.

A CIP record for this book is available from the British Library. US Library of Congress CIP data has been applied for.

ISBN: 978 1 80065 422 8

Printed in China

Editor: Robin Gurdon
Designer: Jerry Goldie
Photographer: Geoff Dann
Stylist: Trina Dalziel
Production manager: Gordana Simakovic

The authorised representative in the EEA is Authorised Rep Compliance Ltd., Ground Floor. 71 Lower Baggot Street, Dublin, D01 P593, Ireland
www.arccompliance.com

CONTENTS

Introduction 4
Basic Techniques 6

LAND
1 **RACING CAR** 10
2 **CABRIOLET** 14
3 **CLASSIC CAR** 16
4 **MOTORBIKE** 20
5 **DUMP TRUCK** 24
6 **AMBULANCE** 26
7 **DOUBLE DECKER** 28
8 **TRAM** 30
9 **BULLET TRAIN** 34
10 **UNDERGROUND TRAIN** 38

AIR
11 **AIRLINER** 42
12 **CONCORDE** 46
13 **BALLOON** 48
14 **SPACESHIP** 50
15 **APOLLO 11** 52
16 **SPACE SHUTTLE** 54
17 **ROCKET** 56
18 **UFO** 60
19 **CABLE CAR** 62

SEA
20 **CRUISE SHIP** 66
21 **GONDOLA** 70
22 **SUBMARINE** 74
23 **PIRATE SHIP** 76
24 **YACHT** 80
25 **SUBMERSIBLE** 82
26 **ROWING BOAT** 84
27 **RAFT** 88
28 **HOVERCRAFT** 90

AND BEYOND
29 **ELEPHANT** 96
30 **CINDERELLA COACH** 102
31 **DOG SLED** 108
32 **SNOWMOBILE** 112
33 **BICYCLE** 116
34 **STORK** 120
35 **CAMEL** 124

Index and Acknowledgments 128

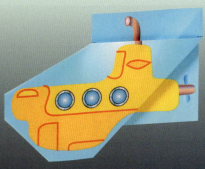

INTRODUCTION

Origami, the art of folding paper, has long been a traditional activity for Japanese children. Most learn the techniques from their parents and grandparents, or perhaps their kindergarten teacher. It is an art that has been handed down from mother to child over countless generations. Nowadays, many children are surprised by origami, saying it is "Just like magic!" It is also highly appreciated by parents because, unlike electronic games, it helps develop concentration and gives children a feeling of accomplishment.

The great pleasure of origami is seeing the huge variety of forms that can be created from a single piece of paper. Every fold makes a different shape, and this variety can be enhanced even more by the combination of different colors, patterns, and types of paper. There is also no need for any special tools or workshops: origami is what anyone wants to make, wherever they want to make it.

The traditional models of origami show beautiful Japanese-style birds and animals, including the flying crane, or traditional objects like the Samurai helmet. In addition, though, any object can be created with origami. In this book I have used traditional Japanese origami techniques to make a selection of vehicles. As with any origami model, they can appear complicated to create. However, by carefully following the step-by-step photography and instructions they are all easily achievable with a little care.

Amongst the projects there are a lot of simple models that will be a lot of fun for children to make with their friends. With the help of an adult the more difficult models will also be easy to make and will ensure a great sense of achievement.

So follow the instructions and discover how origami can create a racing car, airplanes, a variety of spaceships, submarines, a classic car, a double-decker bus, a pirate ship, and even a camel. I hope you will enjoy the extraordinary world of origami through the range of vehicles that you can create using just one or two pieces of paper.

BASIC TECHNIQUES

The most basic skill of origami is folding paper precisely and creating strong, straight creases. This can be achieved through concentration and ensuring folded edges and corners match perfectly before firming up creases. To build up models, more complicated folds are needed to ensure the paper retains its shape. The four most basic of these are explained here.

INSIDE FOLD

Use this technique to surround one part of the sheet of paper with the rest, enclosing much of the fold between the outer parts of the sheet beneath the fold line.

1. Make a fold, here from corner to corner, and then turn down one corner at the intended final angle below the main crease.

2. Lift the sheet and open out the corner that was folded over, then push down the outer point of the edge, reversing the crease.

3. When the sheet is flattened, the folded corner will be inside the paper with the reverse of the design showing.

OUTSIDE FOLD

Use this technique to enclose the majority of a sheet with one folded corner, pushing the folded tip over the main crease line.

1. Make a fold across the paper, turning the tip over and beyond the fold line.

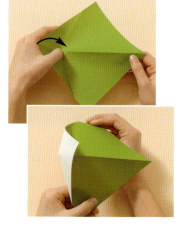

2. Open out the sheet and fold the corner of the paper up and backward, reversing the creases.

3. When the sheet is flattened, the folded corner will be outside the paper with the reverse of the design showing.

SQUARE FOLD

This technique creates a square or diamond shape that can be used as the basis for any number of origami models.

1 Fold the paper from corner to corner then fold the triangle in half again, making a right-angled triangle.

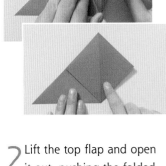

2 Lift the top flap and open it out, pushing the folded corner away from you, opening the crease, and refolding with two new side folds into a diamond shape.

3 Turn the paper over and lift up the other triangular flap, refolding it in the same way so that you are left with a small square or diamond shape.

TRIANGLE FOLD

In contrast to the square fold, the triangle fold starts with a square shape and converts it into a triangle.

1 Fold the paper from side to side then fold it in half again, making a square.

2 Lift the top flap and open it out, pushing the folded corner away from you, opening the crease, and refolding into a triangle with two new side folds and a horizontal top.

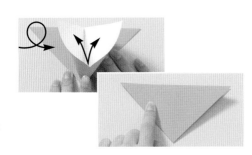

3 Turn the paper over and lift up the other triangular flap, refolding it in the same way so that you are left with a triangle.

KEY TO ARROWS

FOLD
Fold the part of the paper shown in this direction.

FOLDING DIRECTION
Fold the entire paper over in this direction.

OPEN OUT
Open out and refold the paper over in the direction shown.

CHANGE THE POSITION
Spin the paper 90° in the direction of the arrows.

CHANGE THE POSITION
Spin the paper through 180°.

TURN OVER
Turn the paper over.

MAKE A CREASE
Fold the paper over in the direction of the arrow, then open it out again.

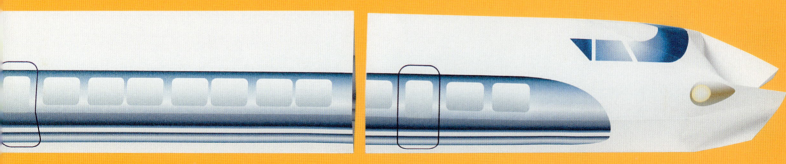

LAND

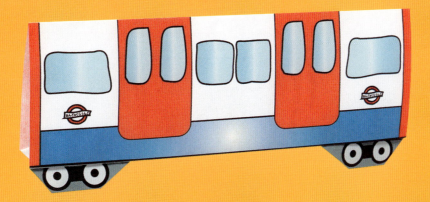

1 RACING CAR

Difficulty rating: ● ● ○

With every sort of vehicle to choose from, why not start your journey into origami transport with a racing car? It's fast and cool and can hold its own in any contest. Making origami models is all about precision, so be careful to make all your creases sharp and straight and always fold the paper evenly. Following these simple rules will take you a long way in origami.

You will need:
One sheet of 6 in (15 cm) square paper

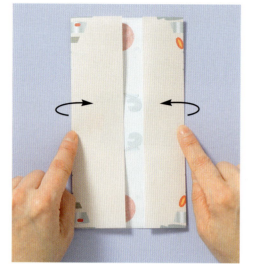

1 With the colored side down, fold the two ends in toward the center to form two differently sized flaps, making creases just beyond the outside of the wheels on the design.

2 Fold the top edge down to sit on the bottom, then fold the upper flap back up to the top to make a crease.

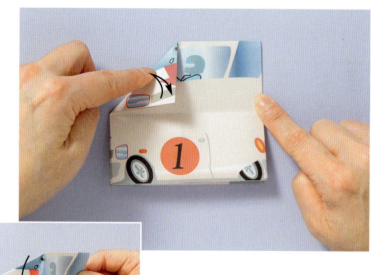

3 Fold over the top left corner so that the edge lies along the crease just made, and press down the new diagonal crease. Open up the model and refold the corner inside, reversing the direction of the creases where necessary.

4 Turn the upper flap back up to the top before turning it back down, making a new fold just above the roundel. Repeat on the other side.

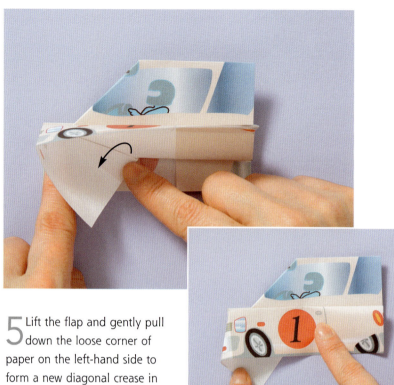

5 Lift the flap and gently pull down the loose corner of paper on the left-hand side to form a new diagonal crease in front of the wheel.

6 Fold the new triangle of paper over the model's bottom edge then tuck it inside.

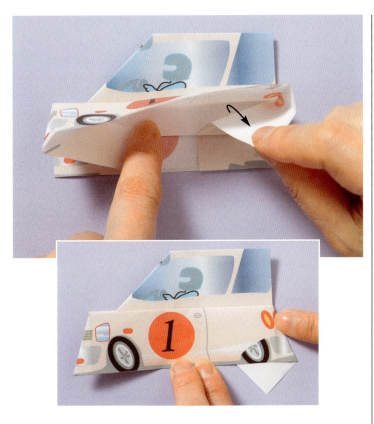

7 Lift the flap again and repeat step 6 on the other side, making a new diagonal fold at the back of the model.

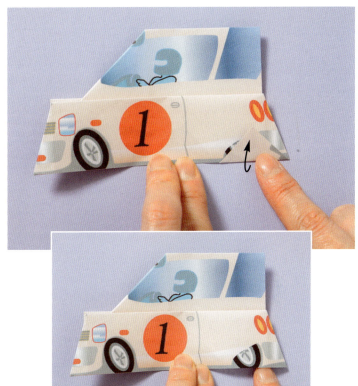

8 Again turn the triangle over the bottom edge of the model and tuck it inside.

9 Fold over the top right corner of the model, making a steeper diagonal fold than on the left, to make a crease, then fold it inside the model, reversing the direction of the creases.

RACING CAR

2 CABRIOLET

If a racing car's not your thing, how about a super-stylish open-top cabriolet that will take you along the seashore with the wind in your hair? It's made in exactly the same way as the racing car except for its folding roof—take care when making the creases that form its shape as they are not all parallel to each other.

Difficulty rating: ● ● ○

You will need:
One sheet of 6 in (15 cm) square paper
Scissors

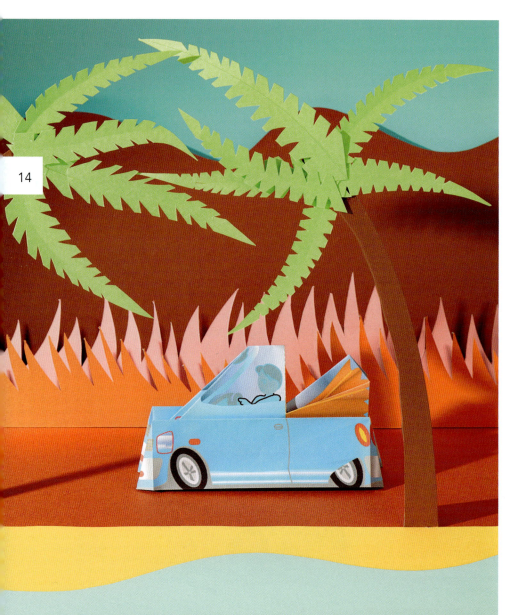

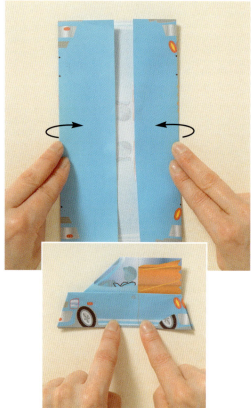

1 Start by making the model in exactly the same way as the racing car (see pp.10–13), stopping just before the very final step.

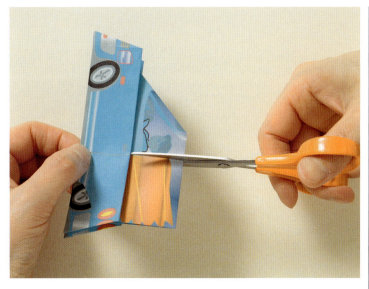

2 Use the scissors to cut through the design between the driver and the roof down to the level of the main horizontal fold.

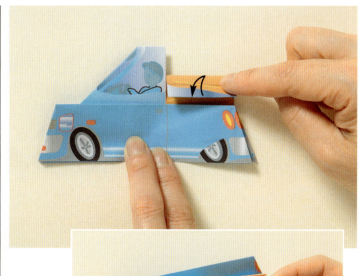

3 Fold over the top edge of the roof down to the horizontal fold to make a crease, then release and make a second crease from the bottom left corner of the roof to the right end of the new horizontal crease.

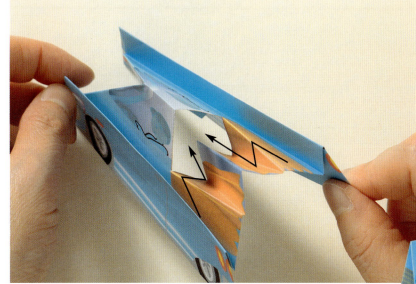

4 Open up the model and refold the roof, reversing the direction of some of the creases to show the car being open.

CABRIOLET

3 CLASSIC CAR

Driving an old car through the countryside can be one of the great joys of the open road. Trundling through the lanes in a vehicle from yesteryear brings back memories of bygone days and gentler times. This origami design is made up of simple folds repeated on both sides, with each wheel housed in its own arch, standing proud of the body of the car.

Difficulty rating: ● ● ○

You will need:
One sheet of 6 in (15 cm) square paper
Scissors

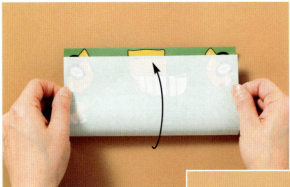

1 With the colored side up, fold the paper in half through the design then fold both edges back down to the central crease to make a concertina.

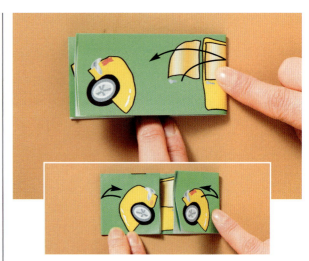

2 Fold in both sides to meet in the center and make creases before opening out again.

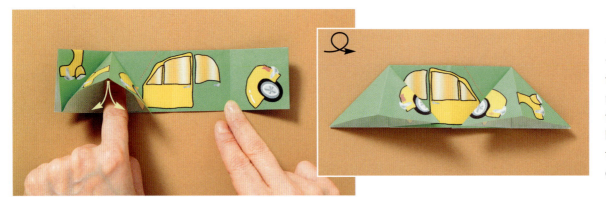

3 Lift the bottom left corner of the top flap and fold it to the right, making a triangle fold. Repeat on the bottom right corner, then turn the model over and repeat again.

17

CLASSIC CAR

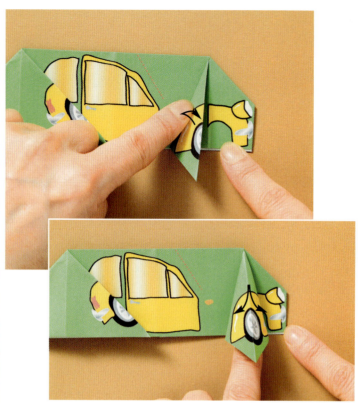

4 Turn over the bottom right corner to the vertical crease to make a smaller crease, then open up the paper and fold the same corner inside, reversing the direction of the creases, and close up the model.

5 Fold over the left-hand edge of the same triangle so that it sits along the vertical crease, then open out the flap and press down.

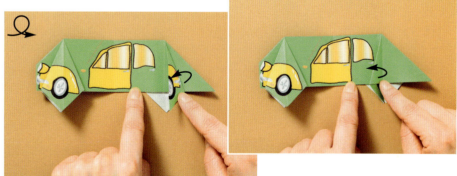

6 Repeat the last step at the back of the model.

7 Turn the model over and repeat steps 4 and 5 at the front of the model. Turn the right-hand edge of the back triangle to the vertical crease and then fold the flap to the left without opening it up.

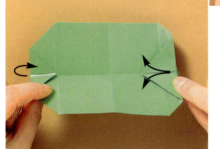

8. Turn the triangle on the right to the left, checking that the vertical crease is larger than the one made earlier at the front. As before, open up the model and refold the flap inside before closing again.

9. Now open up the final corner to reveal the last wheel.

10. Lift the model and carefully cut along the dotted line before gently pushing the hood flat and then prising the model apart so that it stands up by itself.

CLASSIC CAR

4 MOTORBIKE

A motorbike gives you the freedom to travel and meet your friends. This little scooter is ideal for zipping about the city and stopping in the park for a cup of coffee. The model uses some "z"-shaped double folds that can be slightly tricky to get right, but if you follow the instructions and use the crease marks on the paper you shouldn't have any trouble.

You will need:
One sheet of 6 in (15 cm) square paper

Difficulty rating: ● ● ●

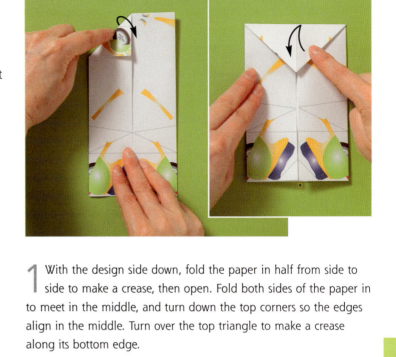

1 With the design side down, fold the paper in half from side to side to make a crease, then open. Fold both sides of the paper in to meet in the middle, and turn down the top corners so the edges align in the middle. Turn over the top triangle to make a crease along its bottom edge.

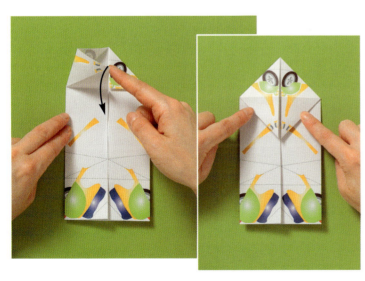

2 Open up the triangle and refold each side of the paper, bringing the corner of the paper down the middle of the model. Repeat on the other side.

3 Turn the paper over and fold back the top tip before folding over the top of the object across the horizontal crease. Ensure that the triangle of paper is brought out from underneath the model.

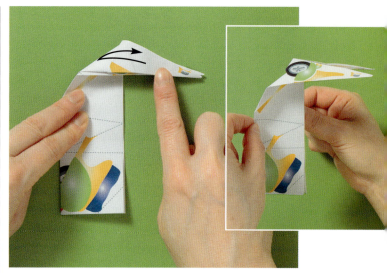

4 Fold over the top of each side of the object making a new fold that ensures the diagonal edge now runs down the center crease. Repeat on the other side.

5 Turn the object back over and fold it in half along the central crease.

6 Turn the top of the model over to the right to make a crease. Open up the model and refold the end outside the main body, reversing the creases where necessary. As you press down, the previously made folds will force the end point downward from the horizontal and create new angled edges.

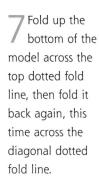

7 Fold up the bottom of the model across the top dotted fold line, then fold it back again, this time across the diagonal dotted fold line.

8 Fold the end back up across the last dotted fold line.

9 Lift the model up and open up the left-hand side, refolding the end into an outside concertina fold, carefully reversing the direction of the creases where necessary.

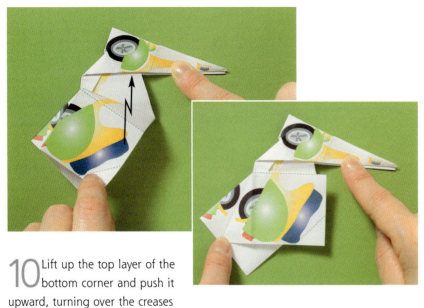

10 Lift up the top layer of the bottom corner and push it upward, turning over the creases made earlier. Flatten the left-hand edge, making a new diagonal crease. Turn the object over and repeat on the other side.

11 Turn up the bottom triangle over the edge of the flap from the previous step, then lift the model, open up the end, and fold it inside.

12 Fold the bottom right corner inside using the dotted fold line. Repeat on the other side then fold in the blank paper underneath the design on the left-hand side.

13 Finish by turning over the pointed ends of the handlebars.

MOTORBIKE

5 DUMP TRUCK

Your origami models needn't just be zippy little bikes and smart convertible cars; you can also make the big, tough trucks that carry heavy loads and work around factories and quarries. This dump truck could carry more than enough to make it useful in any setting, and is remarkably easy to make. Get industrious!

Difficulty rating: ● ● ○

You will need:
One sheet of 6 in (15 cm) square paper

1. With the colored side down, fold in the two ends using the markers shown on the top and bottom edges and crease points. Fold over the left-hand flap so that the crease meets the edge of the other side, and open out.

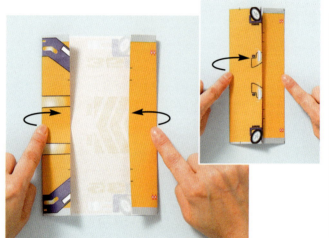

2. Fold back the left-hand flap to make a concertina fold using the edge markers shown on the paper.

3. Fold the top of the model down to the bottom.

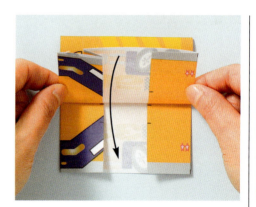

4. Lift the upper flap back up so that the bottom edge meets the top edge, then make a second fold to turn the edge back down toward the bottom and make a crease. Turn over the model and repeat on the other side.

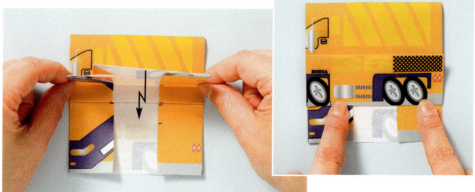

5 Turn over the top left corner to make a small diagonal crease then open up the model and refold the corner inside, reversing the creases where necessary.

6 AMBULANCE

Ambulances are vital across the world for saving the lives of sick people. In every country these brightly colored vans with their flashing red and blue lights ferry children and adults alike to hospital to be made better. This model looks like a typical Japanese ambulance with its big red cross and brightly colored stripes.

Difficulty rating: ● ○ ○

You will need:
One sheet of 6 in (15 cm) square paper

1 With the design side up, fold the paper in half then fold back, using the marks on the paper to give you the crease line. Turn the paper over and fold back the bottom of the paper, again using the marks provided.

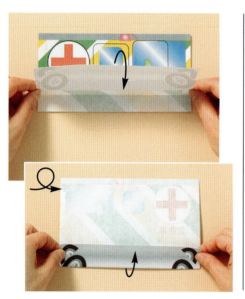

2 Fold over the corners of the bottom flap at an angle, checking on the other side to ensure the wheels are showing correctly. Turn over the right-hand edge of the main flap using the marks provided, creating a small triangle fold at the bottom.

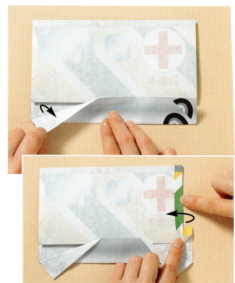

3 Turn over the left-hand side at an angle using the marks on the paper as a guide, then fold over the bottom corner of this new diagonal fold to increase the angle at the bottom of the windshield.

4 Fold up the bottom points to make horizontal edges.

27

AMBULANCE

7 DOUBLE DECKER

London is famous for the bright red double-decker buses that transport people all across the big city. If you sit on the top deck and look out of the front, you will see everything laid out below you as you zoom through the crowded streets. This model is incredibly easy to make, so you could soon have your own fleet of buses to take you anywhere you want to go!

Difficulty rating: ● ○ ○

You will need:
One sheet of 6 in (15 cm) square paper
Scissors

1 With the design side down, fold the paper in half from top to bottom then fold it in half from side to side to make a crease. Open up the last fold and refold the left-hand side to the crease.

2 Open up again and refold to the new left-hand crease, then lift the flap and open it up, pressing it flat and creating a new triangle fold at the top. Repeat all these steps on the right-hand side.

3 Cut two small slits just inside the wheels on each side.

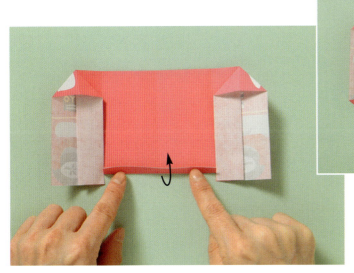

4 Fold up the bottom edge inside the cut slits, then fold over the remaining corners at an angle around the wheels.

DOUBLE DECKER

8 TRAM

Lots of cities across the world have trams that whizz through the streets on special rails set into the road. They look a bit like a train but you use them in exactly the same way as a bus, jumping onto them from a stop on the side of the road. Like a train, though, they often have two carriages joined together and bend in the middle. This model recreates this just with a simple cut of some scissors.

You will need:
One sheet of 6 in (15 cm) square paper
Scissors

Difficulty rating: ● ● ●

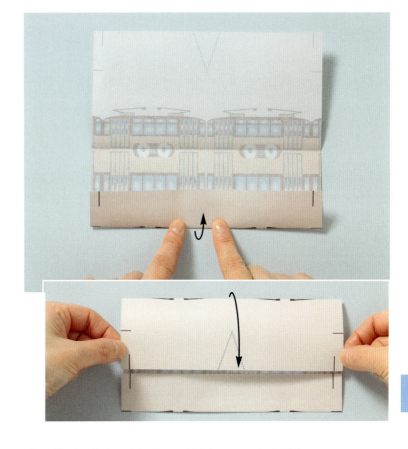

1. With the design side down, fold the paper in half from top to bottom to make a crease. Open out and fold up the bottom edge, making a crease between the marks provided, then fold down the top edge to meet.

2. Fold in the left-hand edge using the marks on the paper, then turn over the bottom corner at an angle to make a long diagonal edge. Repeat on the other side.

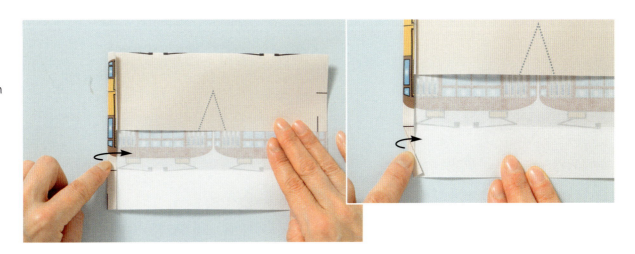

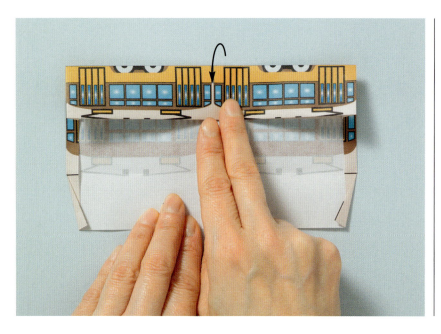

3 Fold down the top edge using the marks shown on the paper, so that it sits on top of the previously folded edge.

4 Open up again and fold the model in half from side to side.

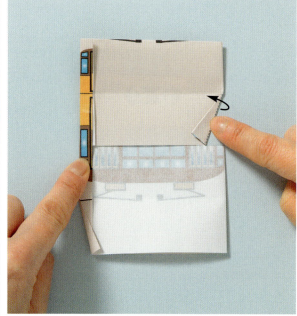

5 Cut along the bottom of the folded edge as far as the end of the printed dotted line.

6 Fold over a flap above the cut using the same dotted line as a guide.

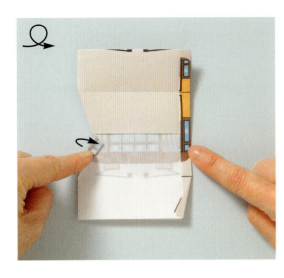

7 Turn the paper over and fold over a matching flap beneath the line.

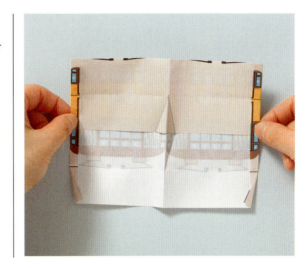

8 Open out the paper until all the creases are visible.

9 Fold over the top and then turn up the bottom edge, slipping it into the gap made by the turned-over sides.

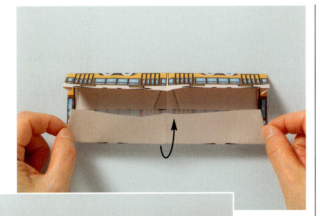

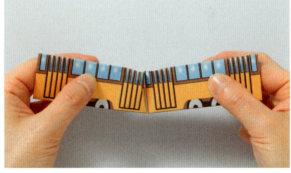

10 Carefully form the triangular shape of the tram, then make it bend by gently pushing in the edges cut with the scissors. The tram will hold its shape as these edges reverse themselves inside the model.

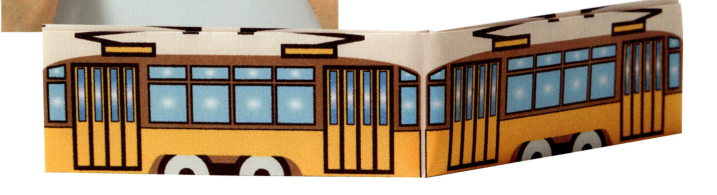

9 BULLET TRAIN

Japan has the fastest railway in the world, with the famous bullet trains racing between far-apart cities in only a few hours. This model shows the famous locomotive with a carriage, and you could make as many as you like to show the speedy engine rushing on its journey.

Difficulty rating: ● ● ○

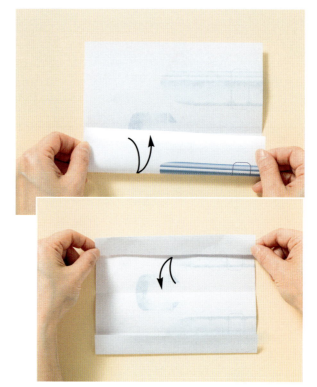

1 Fold the sheet in half through the design to make a crease, before opening up the paper and folding the edges into the central crease. Open up again and fold the edges to the nearer creases.

You will need:
Two sheets of 6 in (15 cm) square paper
Paper glue

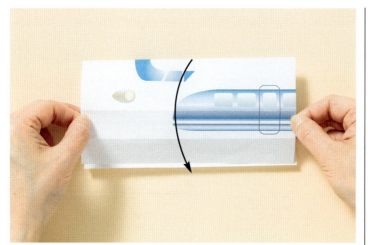

2 Open out the paper again before folding it in half.

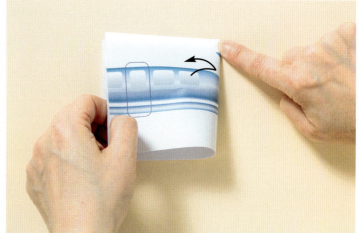

3 Now fold the model in half, making a mark just at the very top of the crease.

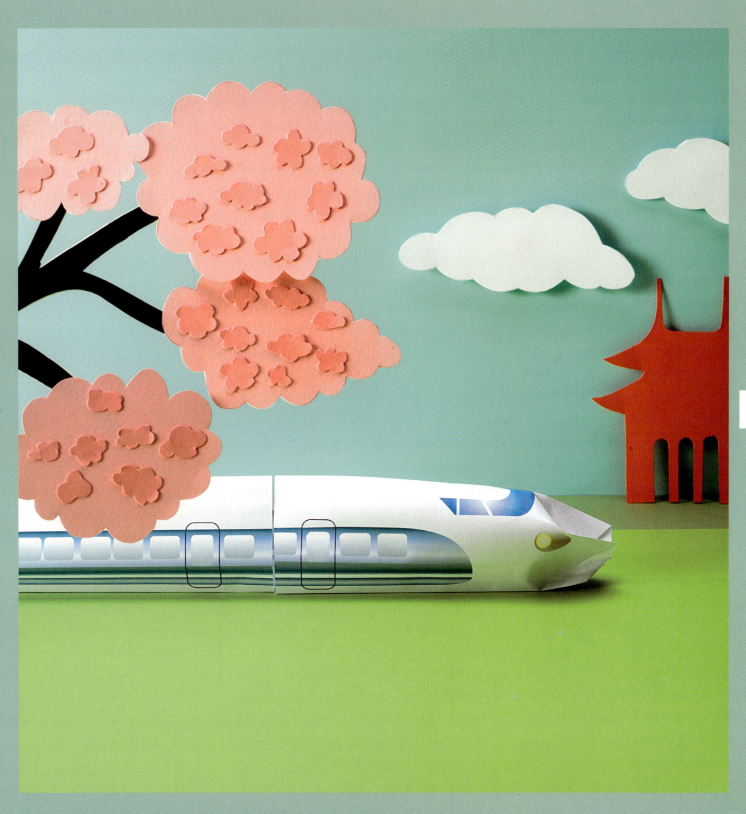

35

BULLET TRAIN

4 Open out the paper and make a diagonal fold from the mark made in the previous step that allows the top left corner to sit on the lowest horizontal crease. Open up the model and refold the top left corner inside, reversing the creases where necessary.

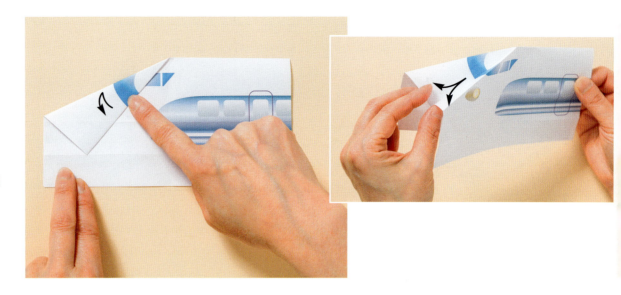

5 Lift the paper off the table and let the two bottom edges overlap each other, then pinch them together with the vertical edges.

6 Turn over the corners of both horizontal edges to hold them in place.

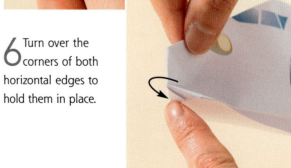

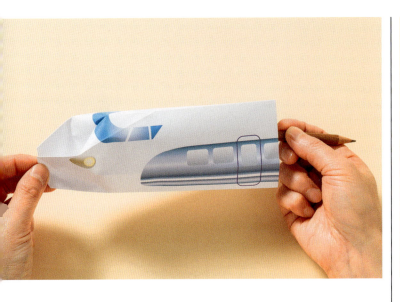
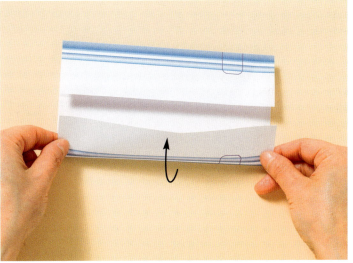

7 Still pinching together the vertical edge, use the end of a pen or pencil to push forward the flap previously folded inside the model to form the train's windshield.

8 Take the second sheet of paper and fold it in half to make a crease, then fold the edges in to meet in the middle.

9 Open the paper out again and fold the edges into the outer creases before overlapping them and fixing them together with paper glue.

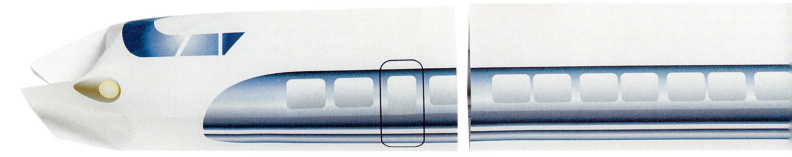

BULLET TRAIN

10 UNDERGROUND TRAIN

Deep beneath the streets the underground trains transport thousands of people around our big cities. Whether going to work and school in the morning or shopping during the day, the trains are full of people going about their daily lives. This very simple model will let you recreate that hectic scene.

You will need:
One sheet of 6 in (15 cm) square paper

Difficulty rating: ● ○ ○

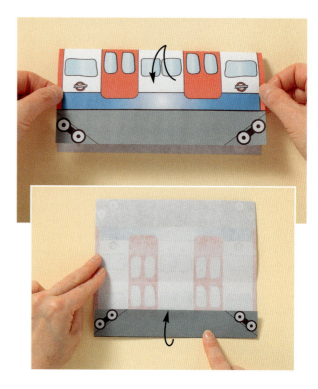

1. Fold the paper in half from top to bottom to make a crease, then open out again and fold up the bottom along the line made by the change in design. Repeat at the top.

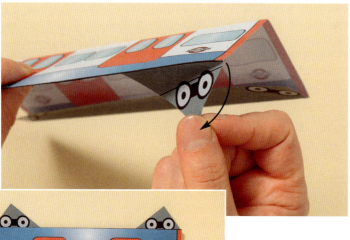

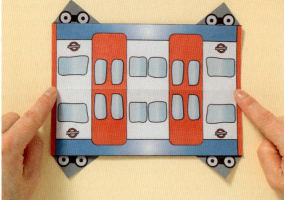

2. Carefully fold down the corners so that the design of the wheels shows beneath the creased edges made in the previous step.

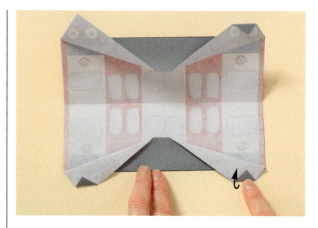

3. Fold up the points beneath the wheels, then fold the paper back in half so that it stands up.

UNDERGROUND TRAIN

39

11 AIRLINER

Large jet planes carry thousands of people between cities all across the world every day. Airports in every country are constantly busy with airliners taking off and landing, bringing travelers on vacation and for work. This is a model of one of these huge planes, and is not only quite easy to make, but also should fly like a dream.

You will need:
One sheet of rectangular paper
Scissors

Difficulty rating: ● ● ○

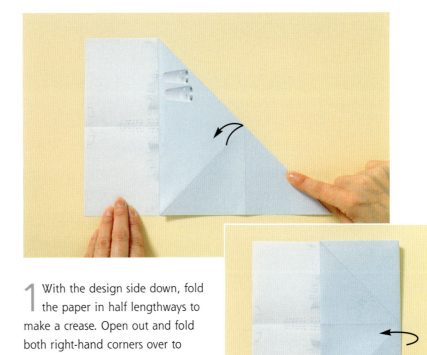

1 With the design side down, fold the paper in half lengthways to make a crease. Open out and fold both right-hand corners over to make two diagonal creases, opening out each time. Fold the end over, making the crease line at the point where the two diagonal creases cross.

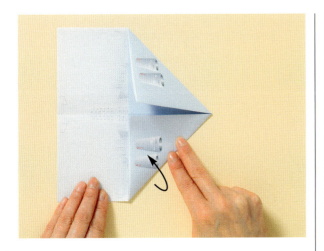

2 Fold over the two right-hand corners to the center line to make two diagonal edges.

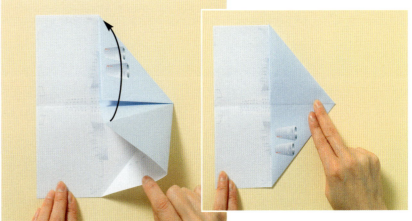

3 Lift the lower flap, take the corner of paper inside, and fold it up to the top point, reversing the creases where necessary.

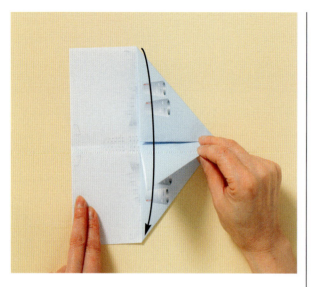

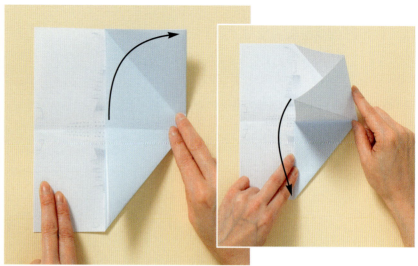

4. Turn this new flap back down to the bottom to reveal the original flap.

5. Lift the upper flap and take the corner of paper from inside down to the bottom, refolding into a large triangle, reversing the direction of the crease. Turn this flap back up to the top.

6. Fold over the outer points of the flaps so that they meet at the right-hand end of the model, then turn over the creased edges so that they meet along the center line.

7. Carefully cut along the center line from the right-hand end up to the edges made in the previous step.

8 Fold both sides of the right-hand point into the slot in the end of the last flap made to create a flat edge.

9 Fold the object in half along its length.

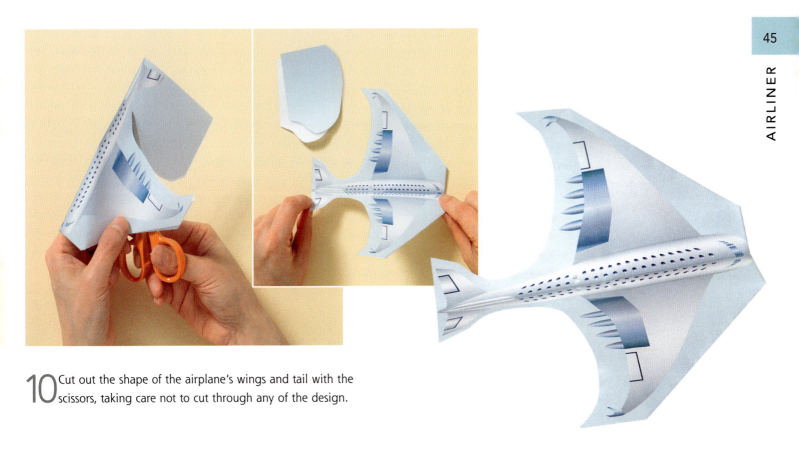

10 Cut out the shape of the airplane's wings and tail with the scissors, taking care not to cut through any of the design.

45

AIRLINER

12 CONCORDE

Difficulty rating: ● ● ○

The fastest passenger plane ever made flew at twice the speed of sound, carrying a few lucky people across oceans in barely the blink of an eye. Now that Concorde has stopped running you can make your own version of this beautiful airplane in origami. It may not be as fast as the real thing, but it is just as stylish.

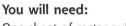

You will need:
One sheet of rectangular paper

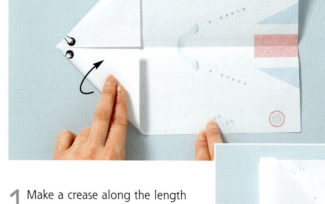

1. Make a crease along the length of the design, then open out and fold the left-hand corners across to meet on the central crease. Turn the left-hand end of the paper to the right, using the marks on the paper as your fold guide.

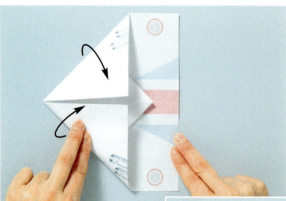

2. Fold over the two left-hand corners again so that they meet on the central crease, then turn the small triangle that is still visible back to the left.

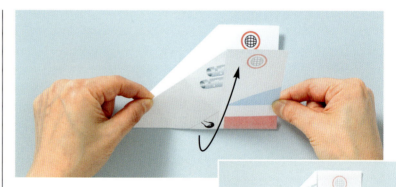

3. Fold the bottom half of the paper up and then turn up the bottom right corner to make a diagonal crease, starting at the bottom of the vertical edge. Release the corner.

CONCORDE

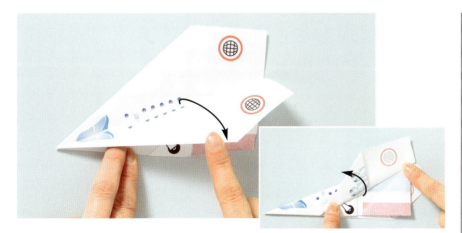

4 Turn over the upper flap so that the top edge runs along the model's horizontal base, before turning the edge up again to create the wing. Repeat on the other side.

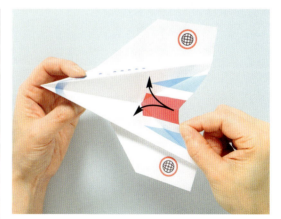

5 Open out the model and create the tail by refolding the bottom right corner inside, reversing the creases where necessary.

13 BALLOON

Difficulty rating: ● ○ ○

Sometimes the best origami models are the simplest, and this lovely model is certainly one of them. This beautiful hot-air balloon could be soaring almost silent through the summer sky, looking down on the world below as it slowly travels across the landscape. With just a few simple folds you can recreate the magic of balloon flight. Perhaps you can make a whole fleet?

You will need:
One sheet of 6 in (15 cm) square paper

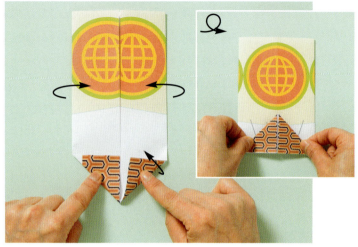

1 With the colored side down, fold the edges in to meet in the middle then turn up the bottom corners so that the bottom edges also meet along the middle. Turn the paper over and fold up the bottom triangle.

2 Turn the paper back over and fold the bottom edges up again to meet along the central crease, then turn over the top corners.

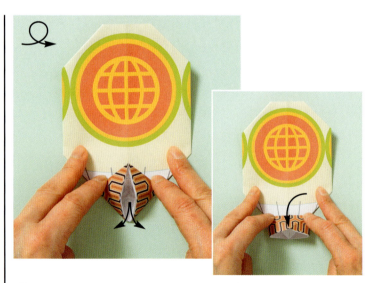

3 Turn the paper back over and gently pull down the top of the diamond at the bottom of the model, opening it out into a square to form the balloon's basket.

49

BALLOON

14 SPACESHIP

The fantasy of traveling through space has been strong for generations. The dreams of school kids everywhere was to travel to distant planets on mega-fast spaceships that could fly across the universe at unbelievable speeds. This model shows how one of those craft might look. With its distinctive shape you can create your own intergalactic spaceship.

You will need:
One sheet of 6 in (15 cm) square paper
Scissors

Difficulty rating: ● ● ○

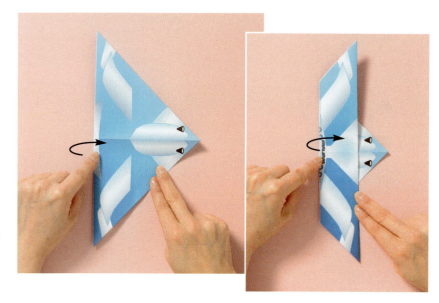

1 With the design side down, fold the paper in half from corner to corner through the design to make a crease, then open up and fold in half between the opposite corners. Now fold the vertical edge to the right, leaving the left-hand point visible.

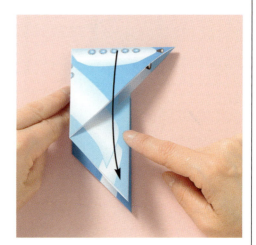

2 Fold the paper in half.

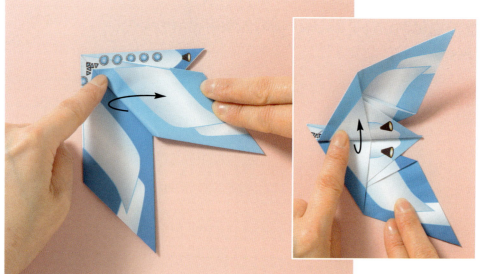

3 Turn the upper flap over to the right at a slight angle from the horizontal and repeat on the other side. Fold the new flap over along its top, angle the edge, and repeat on the other side to finish.

51

SPACESHIP

15 APOLLO 11

The first men to land on the moon traveled from Earth in a tiny capsule, which, after a long journey through space, eventually touched down on the dusty surface. With this origami model of Apollo 11 you can recreate Neil Armstrong's famous words as he became the first man to walk on the moon: "One small step for man, one giant leap for mankind."

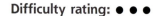

Difficulty rating: ● ● ●

You will need:
One sheet of 6 in (15 cm) square paper

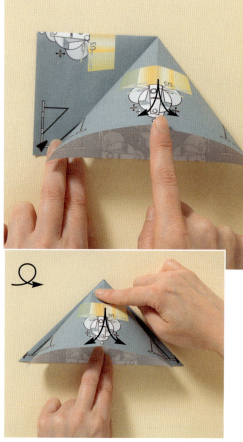

1 With the design side down, fold the paper in half twice then lift the upper flap, open it, and refold into a triangle. Turn the paper over and repeat.

2. Lift the upper flap at each corner and fold them up so that the bottom edges meet along the center line, then fold the same edges back so that they sit halfway back to the crease just made. Turn the object over and repeat.

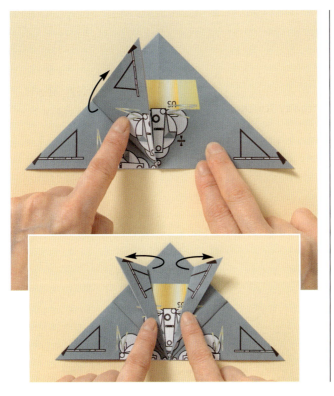

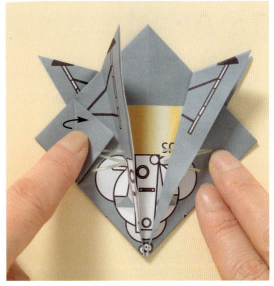

3. Lift the upper flap and fold in the outer corner to create a vertical creases, then lower the flap again. Repeat three times.

4. Lift the object and gently start prising it into the shape of the Apollo spacecraft by pulling each flap in turn. Finish by blowing into the hole at the top to fill out the shape.

APOLLO 11

16 SPACE SHUTTLE

Your origami journey through space can continue with this realistic model of the Space Shuttle. Simple and quick to make, the spaceship can float above your room like the real thing drifting through space. Imagine looking down on the world you know so well from high above the planet, safe inside the cockpit of the shuttle.

You will need:
One sheet of 6 in (15 cm) square paper

Difficulty rating: ● ● ○

1 With the design side down, fold the paper in half across the design, then fold both side points up to the top so that the bottom edges meet in the center.

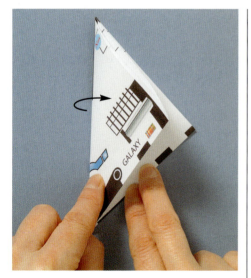

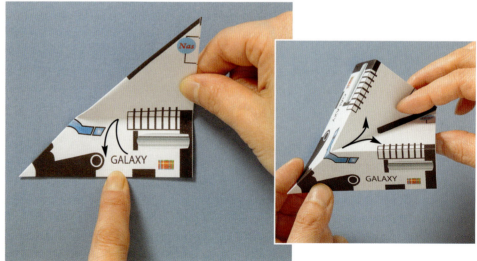

2 Fold the object in half along the vertical center line.

3 Fold down the top point, making a horizontal crease from the top of the space shuttle's windshield, then open up the object and refold the top point inside, reversing the direction of the creases where necessary.

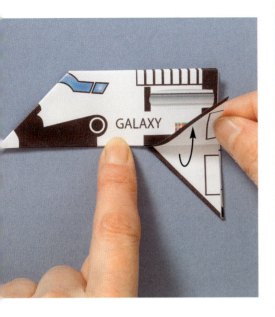

4 Fold up the bottom points to make the wings on both sides of the object.

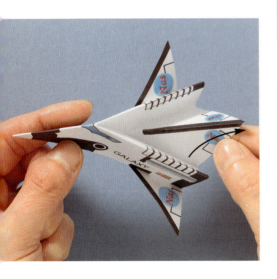

5 Open up the model again and turn up the bottom tip, making new horizontal creases inside that make the tip point straight up as the shuttle's tail.

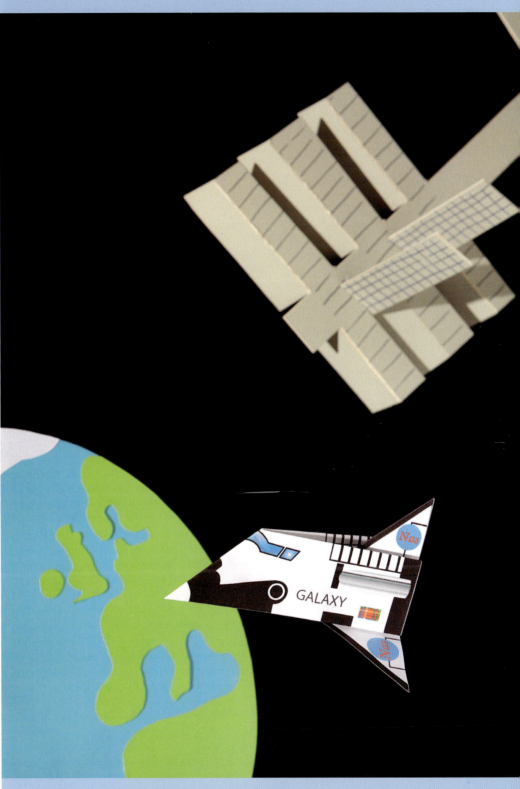

17 ROCKET

Leave Earth behind and fly toward the other planets in the Solar System in your very own rocket. Could you be the first to Mars, or even travel as far as Saturn with its magical rings? Origami can take you as far as your imagination allows, and in this rocket there is nothing that can stop you.

Difficulty rating: ● ● ○

You will need:
One sheet of 6 in (15 cm) square paper

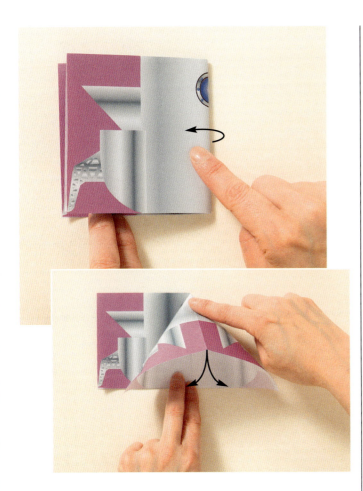

1 With the design side down, fold the paper in half through the design, then in half again. Lift the top flap, open it out, and refold it into a triangle. Turn the paper over and repeat on the other side.

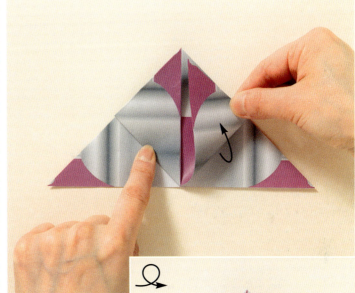

2 Lift the upper flaps of the outer points and refold them to meet at the top so that the horizontal edges align up the center of the model. Turn over and repeat.

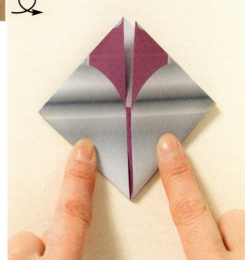

3 Lift the upper flaps, open them out, and refold into squares. Turn the paper over and repeat.

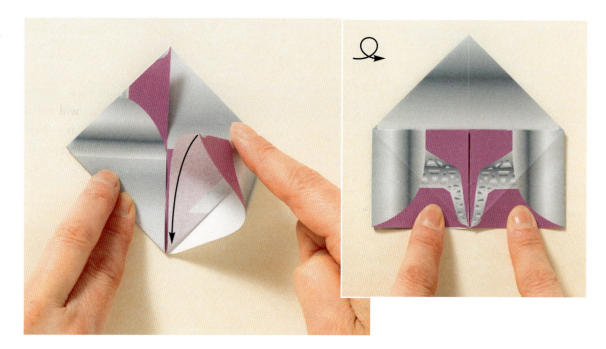

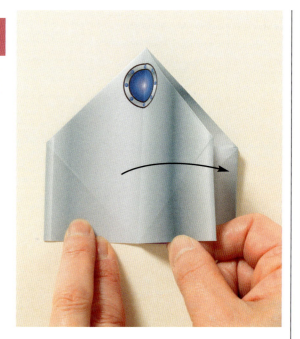

4 Turn the left-hand upper flap over to the right so that the porthole in the design is visible. Turn the paper over and repeat.

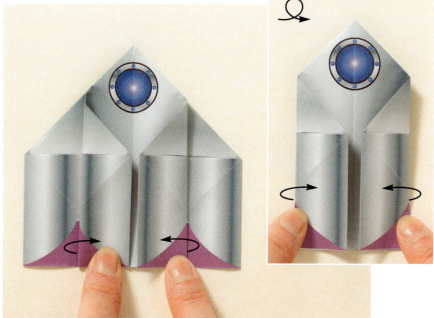

5 Fold in the upper flaps on each side so that the outer vertical edges meet along the center line. Turn the paper over and repeat.

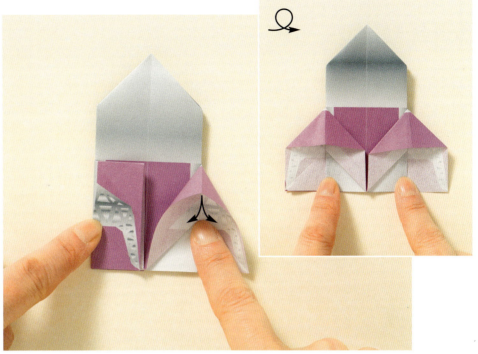

6 Turn the right-hand upper flap over to the left. Turn over the paper and repeat.

7 Lift the loose flap on the right-hand side at the bottom of the object and open it out, refolding so that it has a triangle at the top. Turn the paper over and repeat.

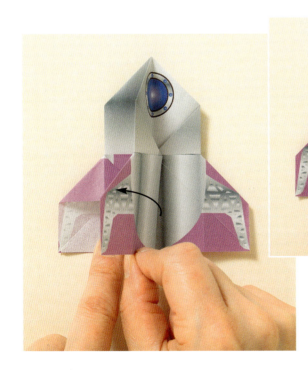

8 Turn the right-hand upper flap over to the left. Turn over the paper and repeat.

ROCKET

18 UFO

Earth may not be the only place in the universe with intelligent life, and the number of people who think they have seen a UFO might make you think we are not alone. Can you imagine an extraterrestrial arriving on planet Earth in a spaceship like this? Do you think it would make it all the way here from a far-off galaxy? Make it and see what you think!

Difficulty rating: ● ● ○

You will need:
One sheet of 6 in (15 cm) square paper

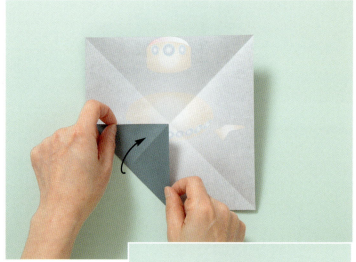

1 With the design side down, fold the paper in half from corner to corner, then open out and repeat in the other direction. Open out again and fold all four corners into the center.

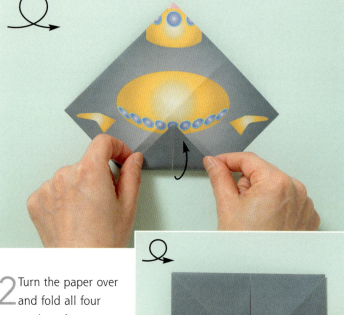

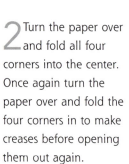

2 Turn the paper over and fold all four corners into the center. Once again turn the paper over and fold the four corners in to make creases before opening them out again.

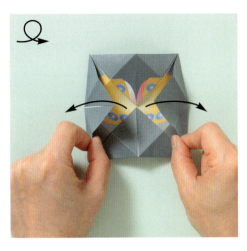

3 Turn the paper back over and fold out the two side flaps.

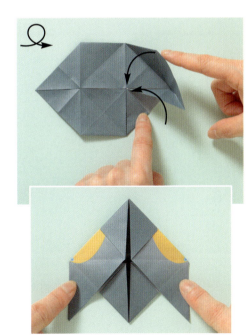

4 Turn the paper over again and fold the right-hand end of the bottom edge over to sit at the center of the object. Next fold the right-hand end of the top edge to sit on the center point as well, before repeating on the other side.

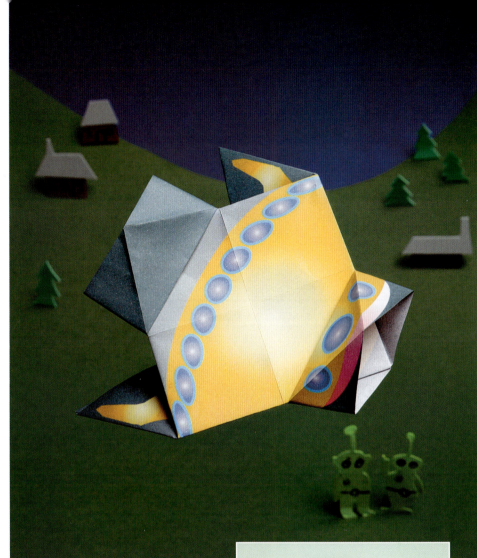

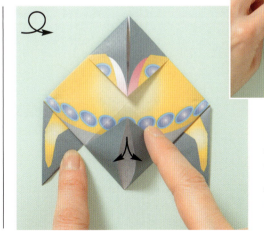

5 Turn the paper over for a final time and reshape the bottom diamond into a rectangle by gently pushing down on the top edges to create vertical sides. Repeat at the top of the model.

19 CABLE CAR

Difficulty rating: ● ● ○

If you ever go to the mountains to ski in winter or walk in summer, you will probably travel up to the summit in a cable car, suspended on strong cables from tall pylons. This model is easy to make as long as you are careful to make the creases exactly the right length. If you do, the paper will fold up easily into the cable car's pyramid shape.

You will need:
One sheet of 6 in (15 cm) square paper
Paper glue

1. Fold the paper in half from side to side both ways and from corner to corner both ways, opening out each time, to make creases. Fold up the bottom point so that the ends of the diagonal crease lines sit on top of the horizontal crease. Open up and repeat on the other three corners.

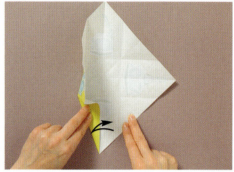

2. Fold over the bottom edge so that it sits on the vertical centre line and make a firm crease only as far as the first horizontal crease. Open up and repeat seven more times.

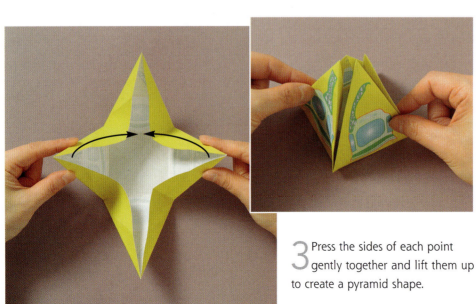

3. Press the sides of each point gently together and lift them up to create a pyramid shape.

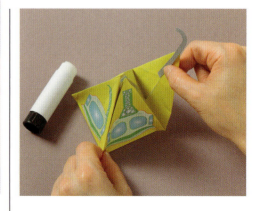

4. Cut a small piece of card in the shape of a hook and stick it with paper glue inside the top of the model, sticking all the other faces together at the same time.

SEA

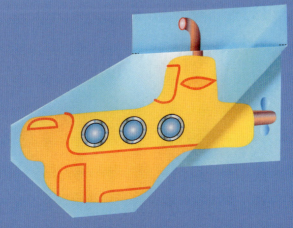

20 CRUISE SHIP

What better way to spend a summer vacation than drifting across the clear blue sea in a luxurious cruise ship? Imagine spending a week with the hot sun above while perhaps visiting a desert island as you pass. Make this origami model to help you dream of your ideal holiday. It's easy to create, just be careful when you make the fold in step 5.

You will need:
One sheet of 6 in (15 cm) square paper

Difficulty rating: ● ● ●

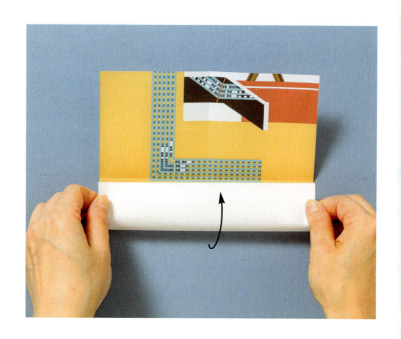

1 With the design side up, fold the paper in half to make a crease and open out. Repeat in the other direction, then fold up the bottom edge to the central crease.

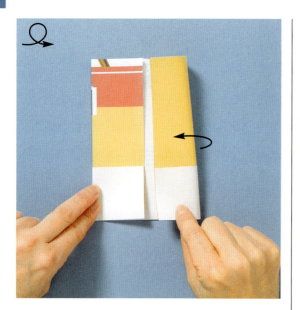

2 Turn the paper over and fold the two sides in so that they meet along the vertical central crease.

3 Lift the loose flap on the left-hand side and fold the corner over to the left, refolding the flap into a triangle that is bisected by the main vertical edge of the object. Repeat on the other side.

67

CRUISE SHIP

4 Fold down the top edge so that it sits along the bottom of the object.

5 Fold the bottom right-hand corner of this new flap up to the left so that the bottom edge runs down the vertical edge. Note that the other end of the model will have to lift off the table to let this happen. Do not try to flatten the object at this point.

6 Fold down the top edge so that it sits on the main horizontal edge. The right-hand end of the flap will form a new diagonal fold and the whole object can now be flattened against the table.

7 Lift the top left corner and fold it down and across to the bottom right-hand side of the object, then turn up the flap's new bottom edge, creating a new fold along the central horizontal line.

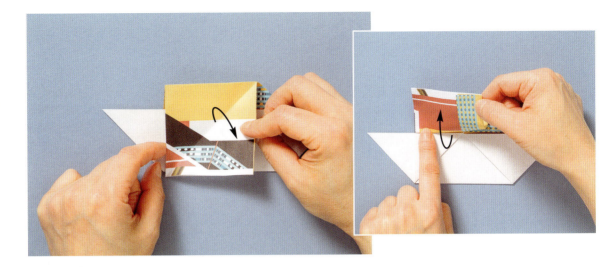

8 Take the top right corner and move it across the model to the left without turning it over. This will create a new diagonal fold behind it, which can then be flattened to create the cruise ship's upper decks and funnel.

CRUISE SHIP

21 GONDOLA

The beautiful Italian city of Venice has no roads, so everyone travels around on a huge network of canals. They are full of gondolas taking people to school, to work, or out shopping. Making an origami model of these colorful and stylish boats is slightly trickier than normal but well worth the effort as you imagine them gliding quietly between the beautiful buildings.

You will need:
One sheet of 6 in (15 cm) square paper

Difficulty rating: ● ● ●

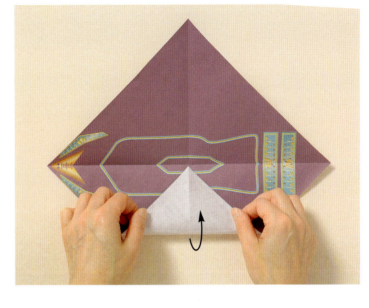

1. With the design side up, fold the paper in half from corner to corner both ways, opening out each time, then fold all the corners into the center point.

2. Fold the top and bottom edges over so that they meet in the center then turn the sides in so that they also meet.

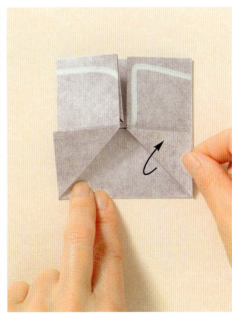

3. Fold over all four corners of the flaps at an angle so that four diagonal folds are created.

4 Lift each flap and pull out the inner sheet, refolding into a triangle that breaks the outer edge of the object. Repeat on all four corners.

5 With the object now in a long lozenge shape, turn it over and fold over both sides to meet along the center line.

6 Turn the paper back over and pull it open by placing your fingers under the edges that meet along the center line and turning them over to the sides. Now turn over the central points to the top and bottom, flattening both of them with a horizontal crease.

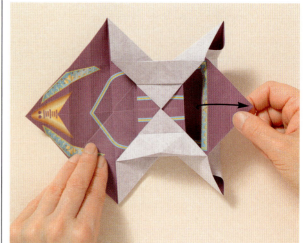

7 Carefully pull open the sides of the paper, releasing the folds in the top points as you go but ensuring the center folds remain in place.

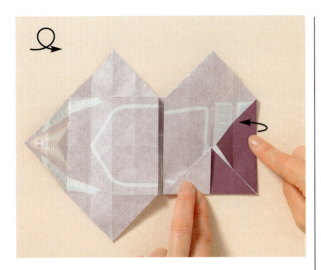

8 Turn the paper over and then fold in the three points on the right-hand side of the model so that they meet in the center. Repeat on the left-hand side but only fold in the upper and lower points.

9 Fold up the left-hand corner of the bottom edge, making a new diagonal crease between the model's left-hand point and the middle of the flap you just made. Repeat on the top edge and then turn over the right-hand end so that its edge runs up the center of the two flaps made in the previous step.

10 Lift up the paper and fold it in half. Carefully holding both ends of the main crease, gently pull apart, creating the gondola shape by releasing the folds in the middle of the model, so allowing the sides to move apart and the prow and stern to be raised.

11 Shape the prow by pushing the end point forward and reversing the direction of the creases, then turn over the model and finish by smoothing out the edges.

22 SUBMARINE

Difficulty rating: ● ○ ○

Drop underwater to the bottom of the sea in this funky submarine—you'll be able to explore the depths of the ocean. It's so easy to make that with just five folds you will be able to explore whatever depths you like. Just don't forget to put up your periscope so that you can see where you are going!

You will need:
One sheet of 6 in (15 cm) square paper

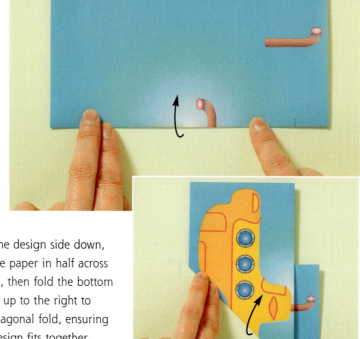

1 With the design side down, fold the paper in half across the design, then fold the bottom left corner up to the right to create a diagonal fold, ensuring that the design fits together.

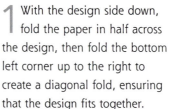

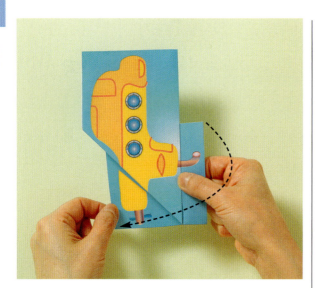

2 Lift the paper up and pull the back sheet down from the original top right corner behind the model, so that the edge runs along the bottom of the model and the design fits together.

3 Turn the paper over and fold over the top left corner at an angle to make a long diagonal edge. Finish by folding over the top right corner. Make sure that none of the design is hidden by the folds.

23 PIRATE SHIP

Pirates have sailed the seven seas for centuries, looking for ships to plunder and goods to steal before heading back to their hideout on a secluded desert island. This pirate ship, decorated with a skull and crossbones, is enough to strike fear into any sailor, and is very easy to make. All you have to decide is if it's going to sail away or be sunk by someone it's attacked.

You will need:
One sheet of 6 in (15 cm) square paper

Difficulty rating: ● ● ○

1. With the design side up, fold the paper in half from side to side, unfold and repeat in the other direction, then do the same from corner to corner.

2. Now turn the paper over and fold all the corners in to meet at the center to make creases, and unfold.

77

PIRATE SHIP

3 Turn the paper over again and fold the sides in to meet along the central vertical crease, then fold the top and bottom edges in to meet along the horizontal crease.

4 Lift the bottom flap and open out the inner creases before refolding to make a triangle on either side of the object, then repeat at the top.

5 Lift the upper flap on the left-hand side and turn it up to the top using the diagonal crease.

6 Turn the paper over and lay it back down on the table.

7 Lift the top left-hand corner of the central square and fold it over to the bottom right-hand corner.

8 To show the pirate boat sailing, lift the bottom point up to the horizontal, but if you want to show it sinking, turn both right-hand points downward.

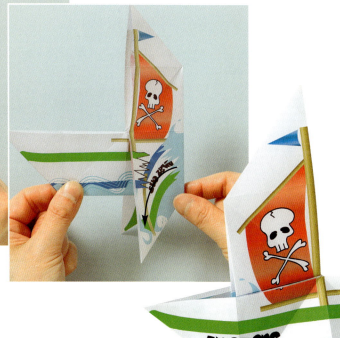

PIRATE SHIP

24 YACHT

Difficulty rating: ● ○ ○

This fast racing yacht could be the easiest model of all to make but is certainly cool enough to stand out from the crowd. The design on the paper is printed on both sides, so take care to ensure that you start folding in the correct direction. Once you've made one, you could make a fleet of boats and have your own sailing races.

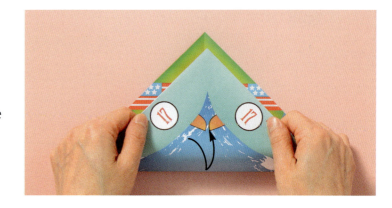

1 Ensuring the side of the paper that is not completely covered by the design is facing upward, fold the paper in half through the design to make a crease, then open and repeat between the two side points.

You will need:
One sheet of 6 in (15 cm) square paper

2 Fold the bottom left edge up so that it runs along the horizontal crease, then turn the paper over and fold in half down the vertical crease.

3 Lift the corner of the flap and fold it over to the left to create a new horizontal edge that forms the shape of the yacht underneath the sail.

81

YACHT

25 SUBMERSIBLE

Here's a project that's perfect for any underwater origami excursions you may have planned. Usually launched from a support ship, submersibles are used by scientists to study marine life in all its forms, whether it's the coral found at the Great Barrier Reef or the colorful fish swimming in the Mediterranean Sea.

Difficulty rating: ● ● ○

You will need:
One sheet of 6 in (15 cm) square paper

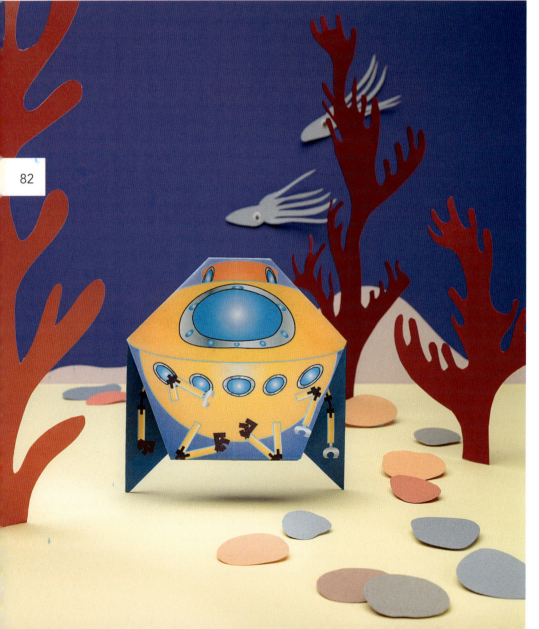

1 Fold the paper in half through the design to make a crease and open out, then fold the upper edges in so that they meet along the vertical crease. Fold up the bottom point across these flaps and then tuck it underneath them.

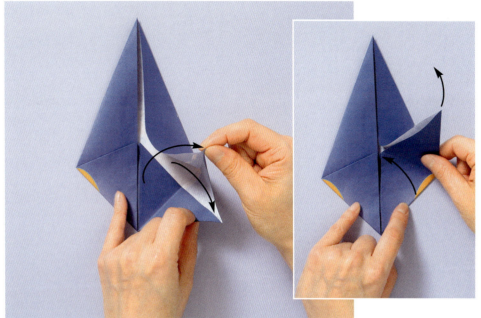

2 Fold the bottom corners up to the center line so that two new diagonal edges are created.

3 Lift up the new flaps and pull out the layer of paper from inside, pressing it together to make a triangle of paper, then close each flap again and flatten the triangle out to the side of the model.

4 Fold down the top point over the two diagonal edges, and turn up the bottom point to make a short, flat edge.

26 ROWING BOAT

What better way of drifting among the lilies on a tranquil pond than a small wooden rowing boat? Pottering among the animals and plants on a summer's day couldn't be easier than in your very own origami boat. Make sure your creases are crisp, as you must use them to pull apart the design at the end and it makes it much easier if they are even.

You will need:
One sheet of rectangular paper

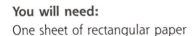

Difficulty rating: ● ● ○

1 With the design side up, fold the paper in half from top to bottom then again from side to side to make a crease.

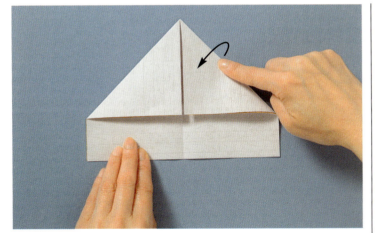

2 Fold down the two top corners so that they meet on the central crease.

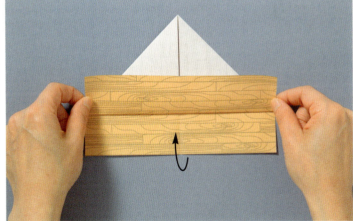

3 Turn up the upper sheet of paper from the bottom edge over the two flaps just made.

4. Turn the paper over and fold the two loose corners over the diagonal edges.

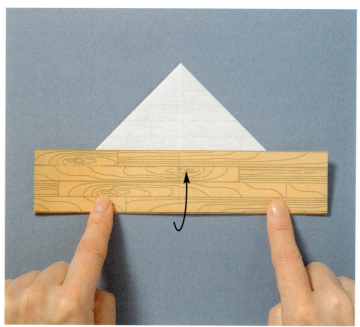

5. Fold up the bottom edge using the edges of the triangular flaps as the fold line.

6. Lift the paper off the table and gently open out the object, refolding it in the opposite direction.

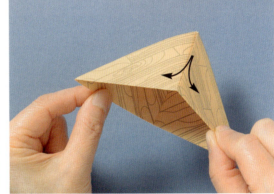

7 Fold up the bottom corner between the two side points, then turn the object over and repeat on the other side.

8 Lift the paper off the table and gently open out the object, once again refolding it in the opposite direction.

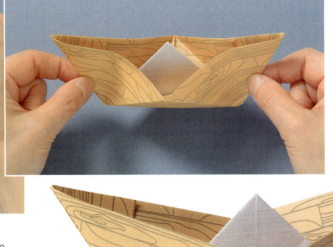

9 Taking hold of the two flaps that surround the inside of the model, gently pull them apart to create the shape of the boat, flattening out the creases to finish.

27 RAFT

Difficulty rating: ● ● ○

Exploring the rivers and lakes in the countryside is best done on a simple raft that you have made yourself by lashing together some logs. In the same way, you can let this origami model take you on a journey of discovery. Although the end design is simple, the model has to be made carefully or it won't form the correct shape.

You will need:
One sheet of 6 in (15 cm) square paper

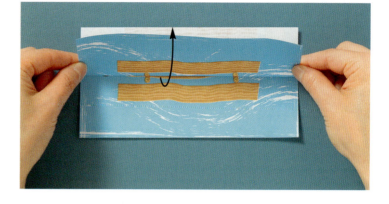

1. With the design side up, fold the paper in half then turn back the top layer so that it ends up ½ in (1 cm) beyond the folded edge. Turn over and repeat.

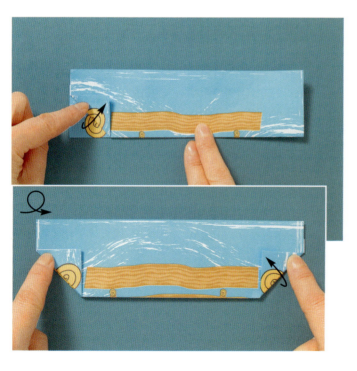

2. Fold up the bottom corners to make new diagonal edges. Turn the paper over and repeat.

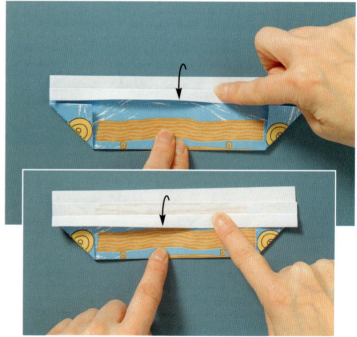

3. Turn over the top edge so that it runs along the top of the two triangular flaps, then turn it over again. Turn the paper over and repeat.

89

RAFT

4 Open out the model and lay it flat on the table then turn over both ends to make creases. Gently pull apart the sides to form the shape, then turn it over to finish.

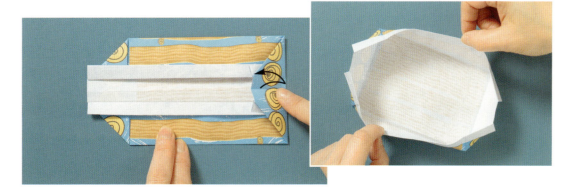

28 HOVERCRAFT

The hovercraft flies across both land and water on a cushion of air, speeding between the two without a pause. This cool model recreates such an extraordinary machine in origami, using an extra strip of paper to create the huge propeller that powers the craft. Prepare to zoom across the sea on a memorable journey!

You will need:
Two sheets of 6 in (15 cm) square paper
Scissors
Paper glue

Difficulty rating: ● ● ○

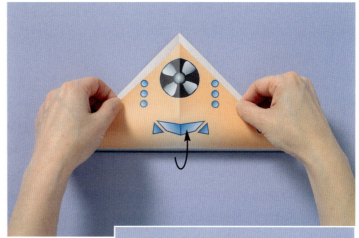

1 With the design side down, fold the paper in half through the design from corner to corner and open, then fold the other way. Turn over the bottom edge by about ½ in (1 cm), using the design as a marker.

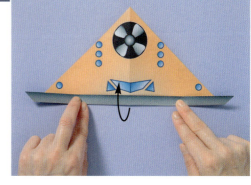

2 Fold up the right-hand point so that the bottom edge runs up the center of the paper making a new diagonal crease. Repeat on the other side.

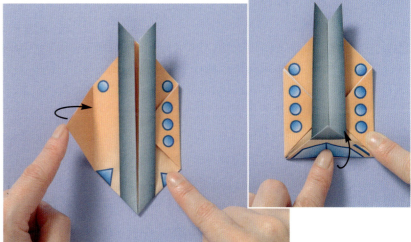

3 Turn in the two sides so that the points slip underneath the folded edges, then turn up the bottom point, making the crease line between the bases of the vertical edges.

4 Carefully open out the model, then turn over and press into shape with the tips of your fingers.

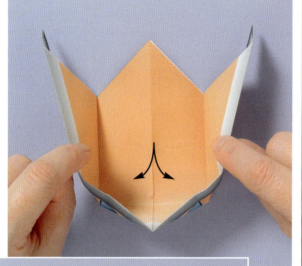

5 Take the second sheet of paper and cut down the marked line with a pair of scissors.

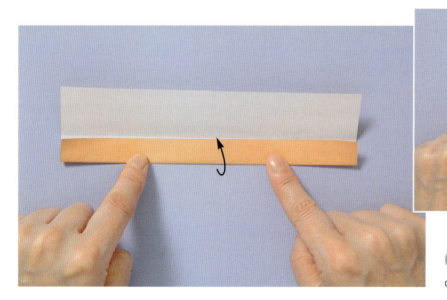

6 Fold the smaller piece of paper in half lengthways. Open out and fold the edges in to meet at the center, then fold in half again.

7 Turn over one corner to make a diagonal fold, then make the paper into a ring and slip the pointed end into the fold at the other end.

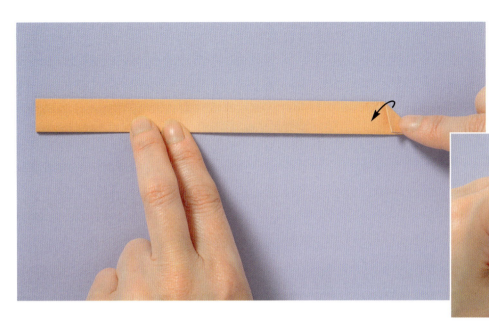

8 Use paper glue to fix the ring under the back of the hovercraft.

AND BEYOND

29 ELEPHANT

The elephant has been an important form of transport since prehistoric times. They helped build the pyramids and carried ancient armies across continents. Nowadays, they carry people and goods in India, taking tourists around the country's beautiful cities. This origami version is complicated to make, but if you carefully follow the instructions you will create a spectacular model.

You will need:
Two sheets of 6 in (15 cm) square paper
Paper glue

Difficulty rating: ● ● ●

1 Take the piece of paper to make the animal's body and, with the design side down, fold it in half both ways, opening out each time, then fold up the bottom edge to the center line and open out again to make a crease.

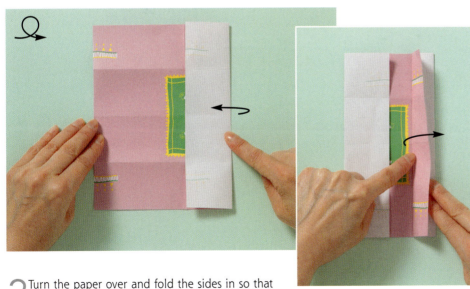

2 Turn the paper over and fold the sides in so that they meet in the middle, then fold the edges back so that they align with the outer edges of the paper.

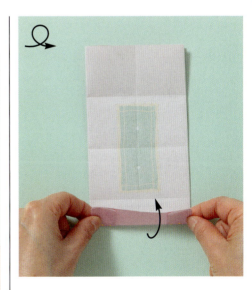

3 Turn the paper over again and fold the top and bottom edges in to align with the nearest crease.

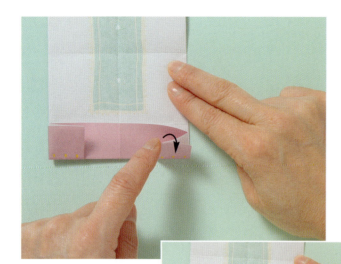

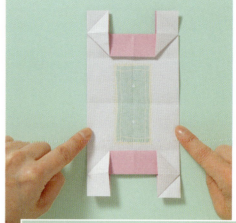

5 Your sheet should end up looking like this. Next fold in half, bringing the top down to the bottom.

4 Carefully lift the top corner of the folded crease and turn it down, refolding the inner folds into a triangle. Flatten and repeat on the other three corners.

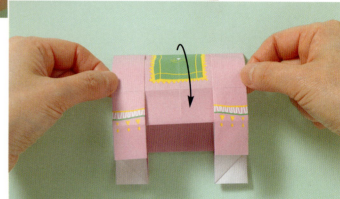

98

AND BEYOND

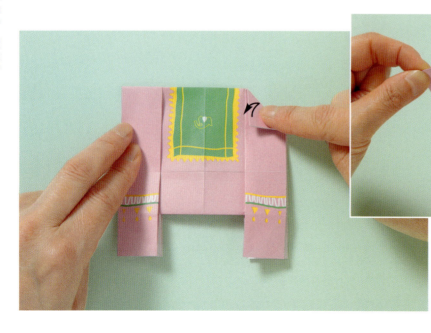

6 Turn over the top right-hand corner of the model to make a crease, then lift the paper and refold the corner inside, reversing the creases where necessary.

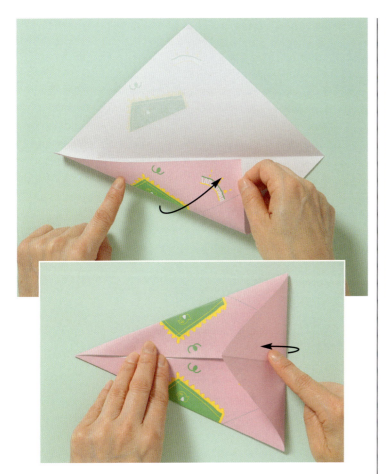

7 Take the second sheet and, design side down, fold it from corner to corner through the design to make a crease. Fold the left-hand sides in to meet along the center crease, then turn the right-hand corner over the edges of these flaps.

8 Open up the paper and fold the right-hand point back inside, then fold the right-hand diagonal edges in to meet along the center line. Next fold the left-hand edges back to the center line as well.

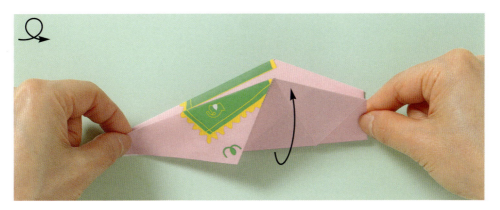

9 Turn the paper over and fold the model in half along the center line.

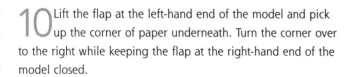

10 Lift the flap at the left-hand end of the model and pick up the corner of paper underneath. Turn the corner over to the right while keeping the flap at the right-hand end of the model closed.

11 Close up the left-hand flap so that you are left with a rounded flap of paper sticking up from the model. Carefully flatten this against the model to create a diamond-shaped flap, ensuring that the central crease is vertical. Turn the model over and repeat on the other side.

12 Turn over the left-hand point at an angle to form the shape of the trunk, then lift the paper and refold it outside the head, reversing the direction of the creases where necessary.

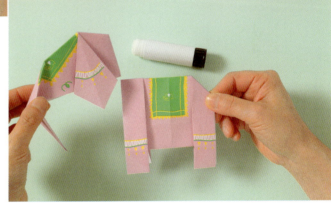

13 Lift the trunk and carefully fold in the edges of the trunk to make it stand out from the model.

14 Turn the head over and fold over the back edge, then reform the shape by folding it in half. Finish by carefully sticking the head onto the elephant's body with paper glue.

101

ELEPHANT

AND BEYOND

102

30 CINDERELLA COACH

Difficulty rating: ● ● ●

Cinderella dreamed of going to the ball, and her fairy godmother made her wish come true when she sent a magical coach to take her there. She only had to be home by midnight, because then the coach would turn back into the pumpkin from which it was made. Your Cinderella coach, though, will be made in origami and will last a lifetime.

You will need:
Two sheets of 6 in (15 cm) square paper
Scissors
Paper glue

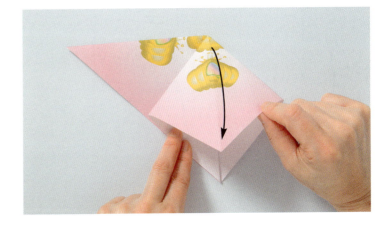

1. With the design side down, fold the paper in half from corner to corner across the design to make a crease and reopen. Fold the other way then lift one side, open out the flap, and refold into a diamond shape. Turn over and repeat.

2. Fold in the upper flaps from each side so that the lower edges meet along the center line, then turn the top point down over the edges of the flaps to make a crease.

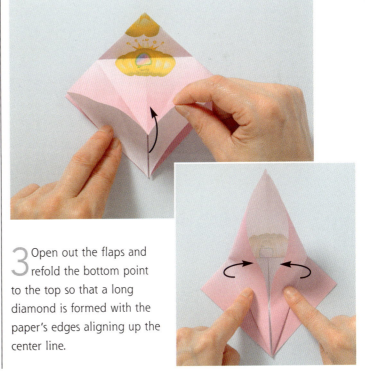

3. Open out the flaps and refold the bottom point to the top so that a long diamond is formed with the paper's edges aligning up the center line.

4 Turn the paper over and repeat the previous two steps to create the long diamond shape.

5 Fold the upper flap down so that the top point sits on the bottom.

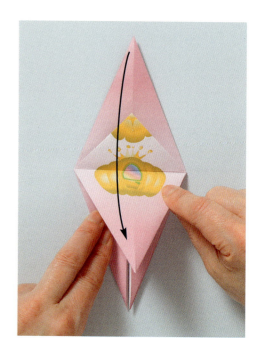

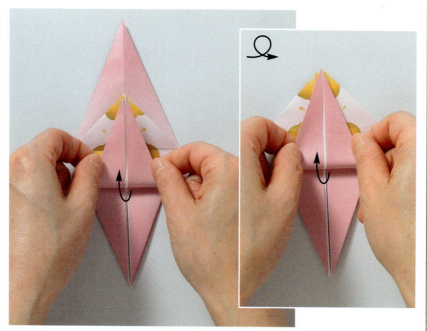

6 Fold up the same point so that it now sits on the top point of the central triangle. Turn the paper over and repeat the previous step before also turning the bottom point up to the top of the triangle.

7 Fold the upper flap on the right-hand side over to the left. Turn the paper over and repeat.

8 Fold the upper flap on the right-hand side over so that the edge now runs down the model's center line. Repeat on the left-hand side before turning the paper over and repeating the same fold twice.

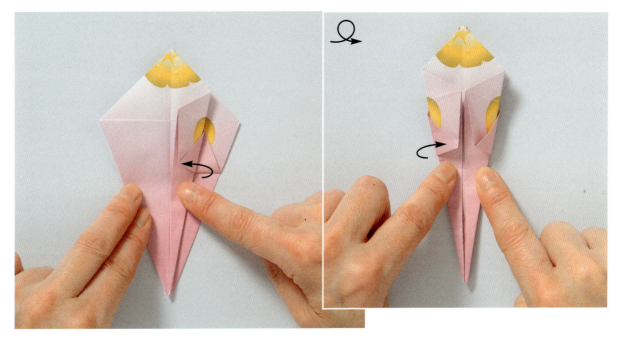

9 Gently push up the bottom corner of the central flap to open it up, then turn it over the edge of the paper before flattening it into the shape shown. Repeat on all three other flaps.

10 Fold the upper flap on the right-hand side over to the left. Turn the paper over and repeat.

11 Holding the paper on the right-hand side, let the other side fall open, then lift the left-hand bottom point up to the horizontal and close the paper. As it shuts, the flap will try to lift. Keep holding it on the horizontal, allowing new crease lines to form, holding it in place. Repeat on the other side, then fold down the two outer triangles at their widest point.

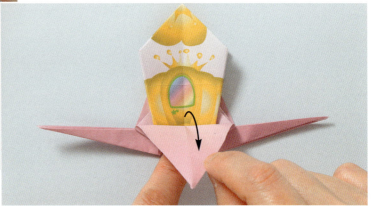

12 Lift the model and gently start prising it open by pulling the flaps apart.

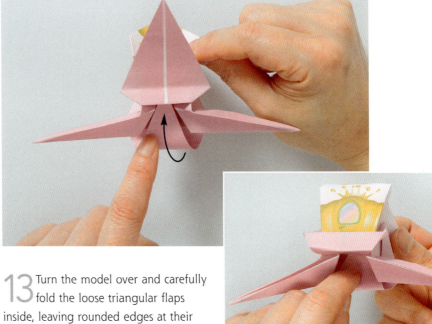

13 Turn the model over and carefully fold the loose triangular flaps inside, leaving rounded edges at their base.

14 Take the second sheet of paper and cut out two small rectangles using the markings on the paper as your guide. Fold each one in half lengthwise and open before folding both edges in to meet along the center and then folding the paper in half again.

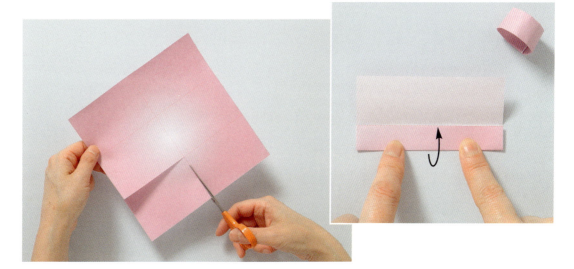

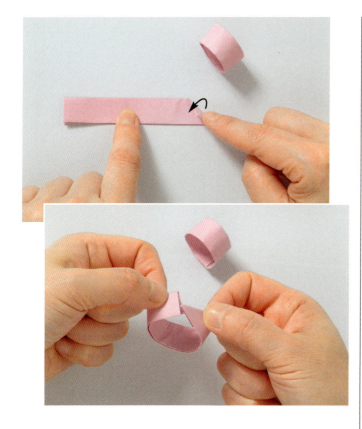

15 Turn over one corner to make a diagonal fold, then make the paper into a ring and slip the pointed end into the fold at the other end.

16 Use paper glue on the underside of the main object's long points to fix the rings in place as wheels.

CINDERELLA COACH

31 DOG SLED

The best way to travel long distances in the freezing temperatures of the Arctic is on a sled pulled by husky dogs. Teams can drag huge weights as they run for mile after mile and day after day through the snow. Check that all the edges of your origami sled are folded over correctly and that you make the straps long enough to go round the dogs' necks.

Difficulty rating: ● ● ●

You will need:
One sheet of rectangular paper
One sheet of 6 in (15 cm) square paper
Scissors
Paper glue

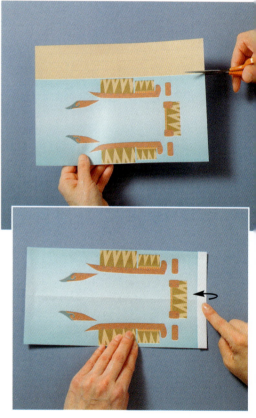

1 Take the rectangular sheet and carefully cut off the side (but don't throw away). Fold it lengthways and open out to make a crease. Take the main part and fold back both ends approximately ½ in (1 cm).

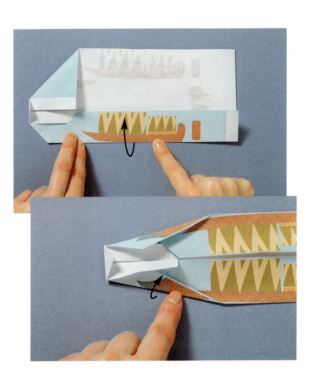

3. Turn over the top and bottom edges so that they meet on the center line. Next make new diagonal folds at the left-hand end between the edge of the folded tip and a point about one-third down the model. Slip the newly formed tip under the small central flaps.

2. Turn the paper over and fold in the left-hand corners so that they meet on the central crease, then fold back the left-hand point, making the crease line between the edges of the small folds in the center.

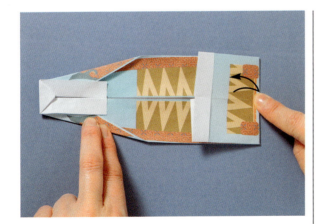

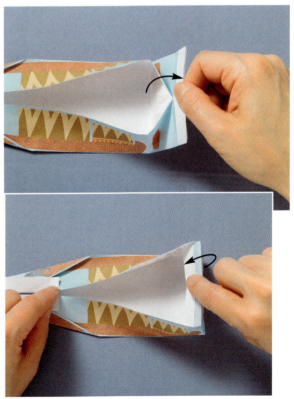

5. Lift the right-hand end back up and open up the model, pressing the edges against the vertical end so that they run along the bottom of the small turned edges. This will make new diagonal folds. Finally turn the folded edge over to hold these folds in place. Put the sled aside.

4. Turn over the right-hand end so that all the design is visible to make a crease.

DOG SLED

6. Take the square sheet and, with the design side down, fold it in half from corner to corner both ways, opening it out each time, then fold all the corners in to meet in the center. Turn the sheet over and fold it in half.

7. Lift the left-hand flap, open it up, and refold it into a diamond shape. Turn the paper over and repeat on the other side.

8. Lift the top flap and gently squeeze it together so that it begins to open up. With your fingers inside, reshape the flap into a rectangle and flatten. Turn the object over and repeat on the other side.

9. Fold over the right-hand flap to the left, turn the model over, and repeat, then fold in both the upper flaps so that their edges meet along the center line. Turn the model over and repeat.

10 Fold the right-hand flap to the left, turn the model over, and repeat on the other side.

11 Turn over the top of the left-hand side at an angle to make a crease, then open up the model and refold it inside, reversing the direction of the creases where necessary.

12 Take your scissors and cut out the shape of the dog's tail from the top of the right-hand side, then cut out the shape of the legs from the bottom.

111

DOG SLED

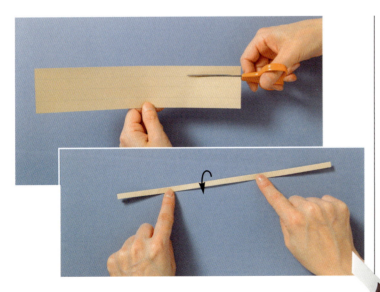

13 Using the piece of paper discarded right at the beginning, cut off a narrow strip using the marks provided. Fold the strip in half lengthways.

14 Fold the end round the dog's neck and stick it in place using paper glue, then fix the other end to the front of the sled.

32 SNOWMOBILE

The deep snow of winter can make it very difficult to travel from one place to another, so the perfect answer is a snowmobile, which uses tracks and skis to whizz across the most treacherous terrain. In the old days, you might be cut off from the rest of the world for months by the weather, but nowadays there is no need when you can quickly escape the worst of winter on a snowmobile.

You will need:
One sheet of 6 in (15 cm) square paper

Difficulty rating: ● ● ○

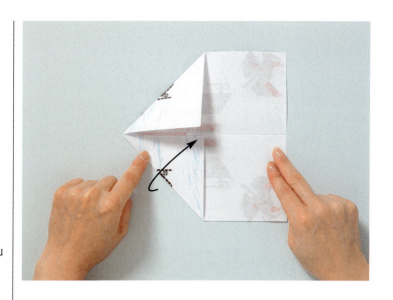

1 Fold the paper in half both ways to make creases, opening out each time. Fold the two left-hand corners in to meet on the center line, creating two diagonal edges.

2 Turn over the top and bottom edges so that they meet along the centre line.

3 Turn the paper over and fold over the right-hand end so that the edge sits on the vertical crease.

4 Lift the paper off the table and fold it in half lengthways.

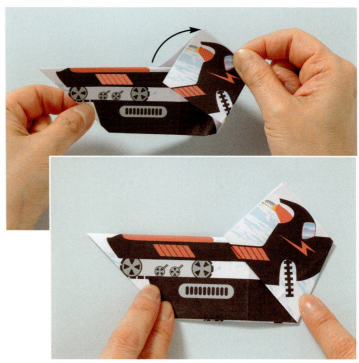

5 Carefully pull up the right-hand flap at an angle, flattening it again when the bottom corner is level with the top edge. This will make a new diagonal crease inside.

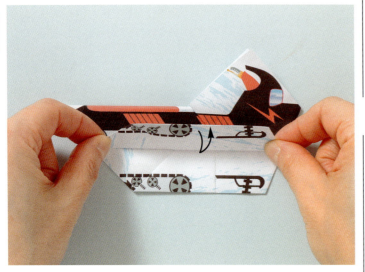

6 Fold up the bottom edge so that it sits along the top of the snowmobile and make a crease. Release it, then turn the paper over and repeat on the other side.

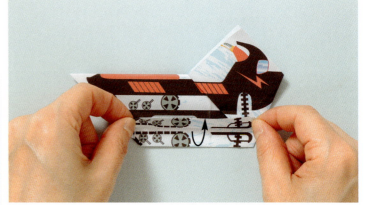

7 Fold the bottom edge back up, this time to the crease made in the last step. Again turn the object over and repeat.

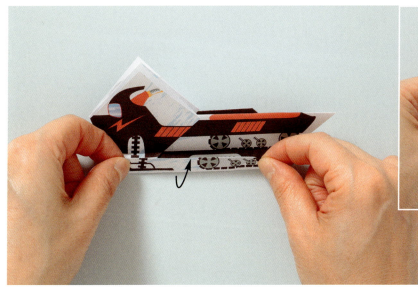

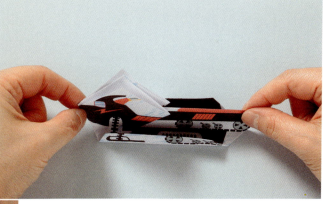

8 Gently shape the model so that it can stand upright, ensuring that the outer edges are vertical.

9 Open up the diamond-shaped flap and push down the inner piece of paper to hold the handlebars open and in place.

33 BICYCLE

Your very own first means of transport might be a bicycle on which you can visit your friends and explore the world around your home. Easy to ride, it can take you down the street or as far away as your legs will carry you. The design of this origami model shows a traditional bike. Make it and perhaps dream about the time you can get a real one of your own.

Difficulty rating: ● ● ●

You will need:
One sheet of 6 in (15 cm) square paper
Scissors

1 Fold the paper in half both ways to make creases, opening out each time, then fold the bottom two corners in to meet on the central crease. Open them out again to form two diagonal creases.

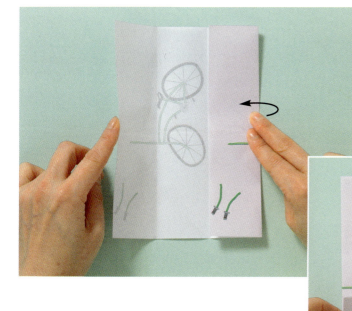

2 Fold the two sides in so that they meet along the center line, then fold up the bottom edge so that it sits on the horizontal crease.

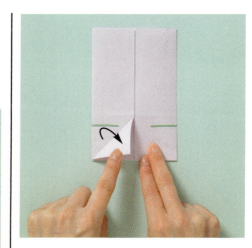

3 Fold down the corners of this flap so that they meet at the bottom of the center line, making two new diagonal folds.

117

BICYCLE

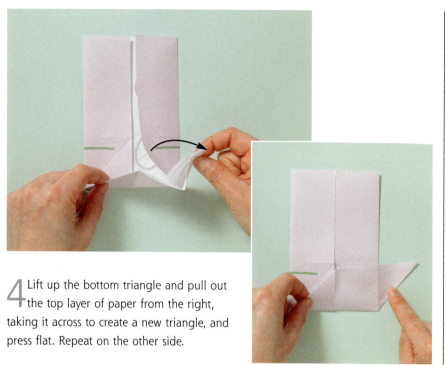

4 Lift up the bottom triangle and pull out the top layer of paper from the right, taking it across to create a new triangle, and press flat. Repeat on the other side.

5 Fold over the diagonal edges so that they now sit on the flaps' horizontal edges.

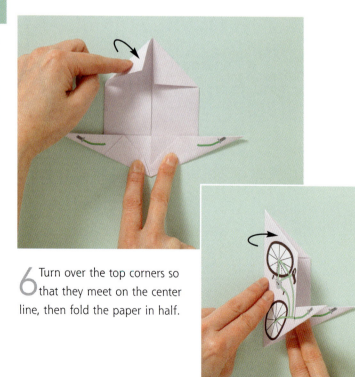

6 Turn over the top corners so that they meet on the center line, then fold the paper in half.

7 Spin the paper around so that the design is upright. Turn over the bottom left corner around the bottom of the wheel, then open up the model and refold the corner inside, reversing the direction of the creases where necessary.

8 Turn up the bottom right corner, then open up the model and refold inside in the same way.

9 Fold over the top points above the design of the handlebars, then give them a curve by rolling them around a pencil.

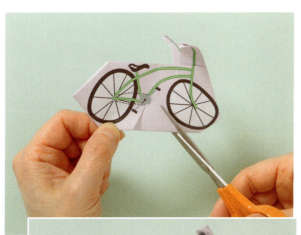

10 Cut two slices into the base of the model inside the design of the wheels, and fold up the flap you have created to make a crease. To finish, push the flap inside the model, reversing the direction of the creases.

34 STORK

Legend has it that the stork brings young babes to new mothers, wrapped in blankets in a basket. Flying through the sky, they leave the infant at its new home, silently disappearing back into the night. The stork is one of the most traditional origami models, and by adding the basket you can recreate two legends in one beautiful project.

Difficulty rating: ● ● ●

You will need:
Two sheets of 6 in (15 cm) square paper
Scissors
Paper glue

1 Taking the paper to make the bird, with the design side down fold it in half across the design from corner to corner, then fold it in half again. Lift the top flap, open it, and refold it into a diamond shape. Turn the paper over and repeat.

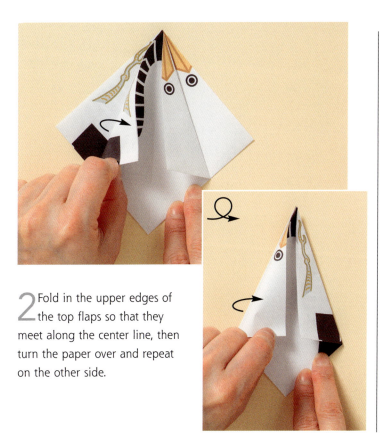

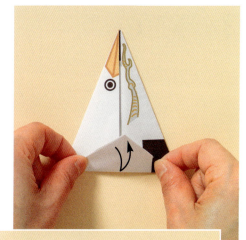

3 Fold up the bottom triangle over the edges of the flaps and release then open out the flaps and pull down the top point to the bottom, flattening it to make a long diamond shape. Turn over and repeat on the other side.

2 Fold in the upper edges of the top flaps so that they meet along the center line, then turn the paper over and repeat on the other side.

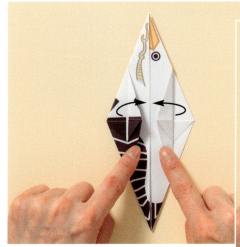

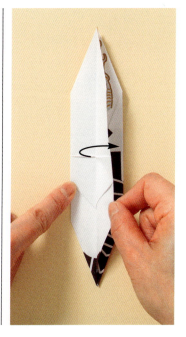

5 Fold over the left-hand flap to the right, then turn the paper over and repeat on the other side. No design should be visible on the paper at this point.

4 Turn in the side points so that they meet on the center line, then turn the paper over and repeat on the other side.

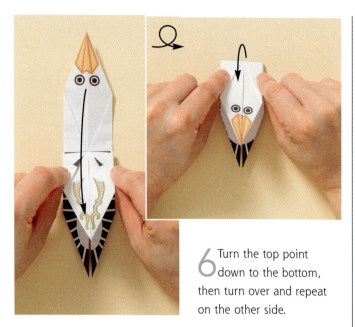

6 Turn the top point down to the bottom, then turn over and repeat on the other side.

7 Fold the upper flap on the left-hand side to the right, then turn the model over and repeat on the other side.

8 Carefully lift the two flaps up and away from the body until they are horizontal. The fold points will create themselves, but press in place afterward.

9 Turn the paper over and fold forward the front point so that the bottom edge is horizontal, then open up the flap and refold the tip inside, reversing the creases where necessary.

10 Fold down the other point to form the tail, making the diagonal crease deeper inside the model. Once again refold it inside the flap, reversing the direction of the creases where necessary.

11 Gently pull the wings apart to flatten the body in between and hold the model in shape.

12 Take the other sheet of paper and cut out one square. Fold it in half from corner to corner, then fold over the right-hand edge so that it runs along the bottom of the paper to make a crease, and release.

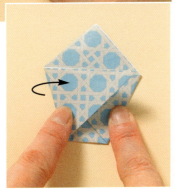

13 Fold the right-hand tip up and across to the end of the crease just made, then repeat with the left-hand tip.

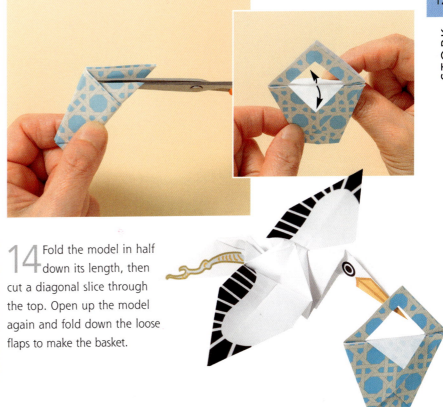

14 Fold the model in half down its length, then cut a diagonal slice through the top. Open up the model again and fold down the loose flaps to make the basket.

35 CAMEL

Known as the "ship of the desert," the camel is famed for its ability to carry its cargo for mile after mile, never needing to stop for water and eating the most unappetizing plants. You can recreate this extraordinary creature in origami and dream of your own desert adventure.

Difficulty rating: ● ● ●

You will need:
Two sheets of 6 in (15 cm) square paper
Scissors

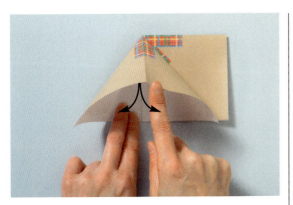

1 Take the sheet of paper with the design and fold it in half from side to side through the design, then fold in half again. Lift the top flap and open it, refolding it into a triangle. Turn over and repeat on the other side.

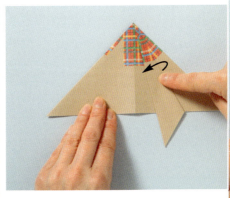
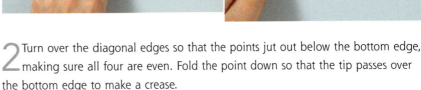

2 Turn over the diagonal edges so that the points jut out below the bottom edge, making sure all four are even. Fold the point down so that the tip passes over the bottom edge to make a crease.

3 Open up the ends of the model and pull out the inner flap, reversing the direction of the creases while taking care not to undo the inner folds of the legs.

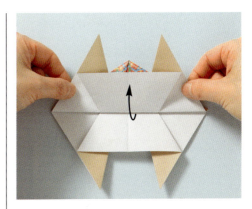

4 Lift up the upper flap and turn it to the top, making the crease between the model's widest points.

5 Carefully fold over the outer edges of the flaps on the legs so that they now run up the inner edges. Flatten the folds at the top, making new diagonal creases. Spin the paper and repeat on the other side.

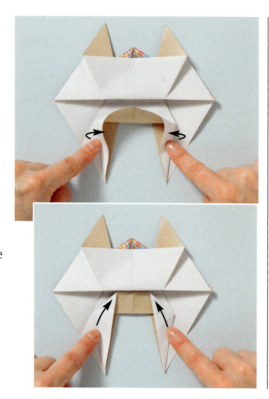

6 Close up the paper again and fold the left-hand outer edge over so it runs along the inner edge of the leg. Release the flap, open up the model, and fold the flap inside. Repeat on the other side.

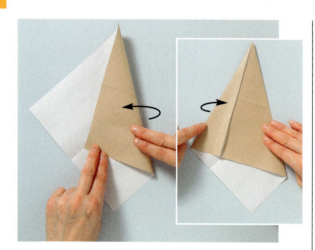

7 Take the second sheet, fold it in half to make a crease, and reopen. Fold the right-hand point over so that it sits on the central crease with the edge running directly up to the top corner. Fold over the left-hand edge so that it runs along the first flap.

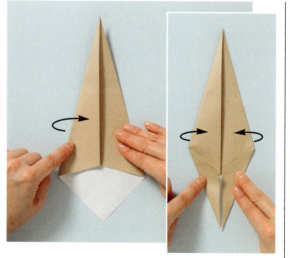

8 Turn over the left-hand edge again, using the paper's edge as the fold line, then fold up the two short diagonal lower edges so that they meet along the center line.

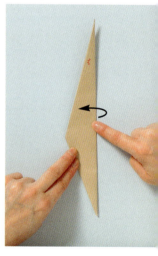

9 Fold the paper in half along its length.

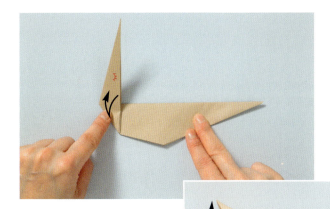

10 Turn up the left-hand tip to make a crease, then open up the paper and refold it around the model, reversing the direction of the creases where necessary.

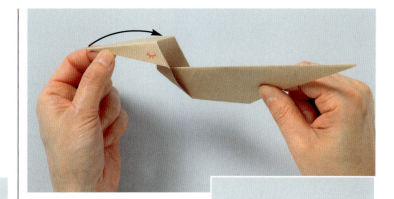

11 Make a second diagonal crease and refold the end around the outside again to create a z-shaped fold. Turn over the end and refold it inside to form the camel's nose.

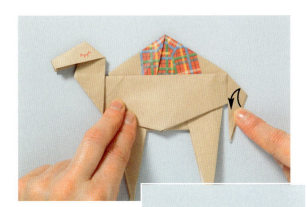

12 Turn down the right-hand end to form the tail before refolding it inside the body, reversing the direction of the creases where necessary.

13 Pick up the legs and cut two small slits inside, then slip the second piece of paper in between the legs and gently push it up until it sits snugly inside the slits.

127

CAMEL

RESOURCES

Origami paper is available at most good paper stores or online, and is available from the author's website: www.happyorigamipaper.com. You can also search for "origami paper" online to find a whole range of stores, selling a wide variety of paper.

UK
HOBBYCRAFT
www.hobbycraft.co.uk
Stores nationwide
Tel: +44 (0)330 026 1400

JP-BOOKS
www.jpbooks.co.uk
289 Kennington Lane
London
SE11 5QY
Tel: +44 (0)20 7839 4839
Email: info@jpbooks.co.uk

JAPAN CENTRE
www.japancentre.com
Email: enquiry@japancentre.com

THE JAPANESE SHOP
www.thejapaneseshop.co.uk
Tel: +44(0)1423 876 320
Email: info@thejapaneseshop.co.uk

USA
MICHAELS
www.michaels.com
Stores nationwide

HOBBY LOBBY
www.hobbylobby.com
Stores nationwide

JO-ANN FABRIC AND CRAFT STORE
www.joann.com
Stores nationwide

HAKUBUNDO (HONOLULU, HAWAII)
www.hakubundo.com

Canada
DESERRES
www.deserres.ca
Email: service@deserres.ca

France
CULTURE JAPON S.A.S.
www.boutiquecuturejapon.fr
Store in Maison du la Culture du Japon
101 bis quai Branly
75015, Paris
Tel: +33 (0)1 45 79 02 00
Email: culturejpt@wanadoo.fr

BOOKS
The Simple Art of Japanese Origami by Mari Ono (CICO Books)
Origami Garden by Mari Ono (CICO Books)
Origami for Kids by Mari Ono (CICO Books)
Kantan Origami 100 part 2 by Kazuo Kobayashi (Nihon Vogue-Sha Co. Ltd.)
Ugokasu Tobasu Origami by Seibido Shuppan Editorial Department (Seibido Shuppan Co. Ltd.)

WEBSITES
Origami Club: en.origami-club.com
Origami Kaikan: origamikaikan.co.jp/lp/english_guide.html
Japan Origami Academic Society: www.origami.jp
Nippon Origami Association: www.origami-noa.jp/
Origami USA: www.origami-usa.org
British Origami Society: www.britishorigami.info

INDEX

A
airliner 42–5
ambulance 26–7
Apollo 11: 52–3
arrows, key 7

B
balloon, hot air 48–9
bicycle 116–19
bullet train 34–7
bus, double-decker 28–9

C
cable car 62–3
cabriolet 14–15
camel 124–7
cars
    cabriolet 14–15
    classic 16–19
    racing 10–13
Cinderella coach 102–7
classic car 16–19
Concorde 46–7
cruise ship 66–9

D
dogsled 108–11
double-decker bus 28–9
dump truck 24–5

E
elephant 96–101

F
folds 6–7

G
gondola 70–3

H
hot air balloon 48–9
hovercraft 90–3

I
inside fold 6

M
motorbike 20–3

O
outside fold 6

P
pirate ship 76–9

R
racing car 10–13
raft 88–9
rocket 56–9
rowing boat 84–7

S
ships
    cruise 66–9
    pirate 76–9
snowmobile 112–15
Space Shuttle 54–5
spaceship 50–1
square fold 7
stork 120–3
submarine 74–5
submersible 82–3

T
techniques 6–7
trains
    bullet 34–7
    underground 38–9
tram 30–3
triangle fold 7

U
UFO 60–1
underground train 38–9

Y
yacht 80–1

ACKNOWLEDGMENTS

My big thank you goes to the team that created this book. I've been extremely fortunate in that a great many people have helped me and to them I say a very big thank you, especially my editor, Robin Gurdon, who has helped me throughout with skill and knowledge. I'm also immensely grateful to the photographer, Geoff Dann.
I also say many thanks to the following: Cindy Richards, Sally Powell, and Pete Jorgensen of CICO Books, as well as Trina Dalziel who styled and designed the backgrounds for all the projects in this book.
My friends and family have also been tremendously supportive, in particular Takumasa, my husband, who has designed all origami papers included with this book.